WORLD BOOK'S

YOUNG SCIENTIST

WORLD BOOK'S

YOUNG SCIENTIST

•STUDENT GUIDE
•INDEX

10

World Book, Inc.
a Scott Fetzer company
Chicago

Activities that have this warning symbol require some adult supervision!

The quest to explore the known world and to describe its creation and subsequent development is nearly as old as mankind. In the Western world, the best-known creation story comes from the book of Genesis. It tells how God created Earth and all living things. Modern religious thinkers interpret the Biblical story of creation in various ways. Some believe that creation occurred exactly as Genesis describes it. Others think that God's method of creation is revealed through scientific investigation. *Young Scientist* presents an exciting picture of what scientists have learned about life and the universe.

World Book, Inc.
233 N. Michigan Avenue
Chicago, IL 60601

For information on other World Book products, call 1-800-WORLDBK (967-5325), or visit us at our Web site at http://www.worldbook.com

ISBN: 0-7166-2760-4 (volume X)
ISBN: 0-7166-2797-3 (set)

Library of Congress Catalog Card No. 00-107193

Printed in the United States of America

1 2 3 4 5 6 7 06 05 04 03 02 01 00

Contents

Student Guide

8 **Are you a scientist?**
A scientist is someone who decides what a problem is and then solves it.

10 **Your *Young Scientist* set**
Find out what's in each of your *Young Scientist* books. Which areas of science do they explore?

12 **What is science?**
How do scientists find out about the world around them?

14 **The natural world of science**
The natural world includes living things, as well as the different parts of the planet Earth and outer space.

16 **The artificial world of science**
We use natural materials to make new, artificial ones. What is technology? Find out about some important inventions.

18 **The hidden world of science**
Many living and non-living things are too tiny to see without a microscope. What is an electron microscope?

20 **The work of a scientist**
What are the three main areas of science? Find out about the work of different types of scientists.

22 **Become a young scientist**
A young scientist needs to learn many new words. Recording information is an important part of scientific work.

24 **A place to work**
How can you set up your own science laboratory? What do you need in it?

26 **Keeping a record of your work**
How can you record your experiments and other scientific information?

28 **Using equipment**
Which battery can you use in your experiments? Learn the correct way to use different tools.

30 **Finding materials**
Where can you find the different materials and equipment you need?

32 **Learning to measure**
How do you measure mass, distance, and time? Why do we need big and small units?

34 **Measuring in units**
How can you measure area? What is volume? What is density?

36 **Equipment for measuring**
Find out about different kinds of measuring equipment. Make your own measuring devices.

38 **Working safely**
Safety in science is very important. How can you do your experiments safely?

Index

40 **Cumulative index**

95 **Glossary**

112 **Answers**

114 **Topic webs**

Staff and Consultants

President
Robert C. Martin

Vice President, Publisher
Michael Ross

Editorial

Managing Editor
Maureen Mostyn Liebenson

Senior Editor
Shawn Brennan

Contributing Editor
Diana Myers

Permissions Editor
Janet T. Peterson

International Editor
Jeff Groman

Indexing Services

David Pofelski, Head
Joyce Goldenstern

Special Consultative Services

Editor in Chief, World Book Encyclopedia
Dale W. Jacobs

Science Subject Editors
Brad Finger
Jay Myers
Thomas J. Wrobel

Statistical Editor
Ken Schenkman

Art

Executive Director
Roberta Dimmer

Art Director
Wilma Stevens

Designer
John Horvath

Contributing Designers
Donna Cook
Sarah Figlio
Rebecca Schneider

Cover Design
Tessing Design, Inc.

Photography Manager
Sandra M. Dyrlund

Photographs Editors
Sylvia Ohlrich
Carol Parden

Production Assistants
Laurie Schuh
John Whitney

Research

Executive Director, Product Development and Research Services
Paul A. Kobasa

Senior Researchers
Cheryl Graham, Coordinator
Lynn Durbin
Karen McCormack
Andrew Roberts
Loranne K. Shields

Production

Senior Manager, Pre-Press and Manufacturing
Carma Fazio

Manager, Manufacturing
Barbara Podczerwinski

Senior Production Manager
Madelyn Underwood

Production Manager
Kathe Ellefsen

Manufacturing Assistant Manager
Valerie Piarowski

Pre-Press Production Assistant
Jill Waltman

Proofreaders
Anne Dillon, Head
Chad Rubel

Text Processing
Curley Hunter
Gwendolyn Johnson

Authors and Contributors
Linda Gamlin
Suzanne Hopwood
Robin Kerrod
Peter Lafferty
Peter Mellett
Michael Pollard
Keith Wicks

Science Consultants (Educational)

Marlene Furch, M.A., science teacher, Decatur Classical School, Chicago, IL

Charles J. LaRue, Ph.D., science educator and consultant, Rockville, MD

Glenn W. McGee, Ph.D., Superintendent of Schools, Aptakisic-Tripp Community Consolidated School District, Buffalo Grove, IL

Peter Mellett, B Sc. (Hons.), Dip. Ed., secondary school science teacher, free-lance writer, Bath, England

Specialist Consultants

Architecture
G. Beard, M.A., D. Litt., free-lance lecturer in architecture and decorative arts, Bath, England

Botany
David Gledhill, Ph.D., lecturer, Botany Department, University of Bristol, England

Chemistry
A. P. Cox, School of Chemistry, University of Bristol, England

Civil Engineering
D. O'Byrne, civil engineering technologist, Bath, England

Communication
D. Wood, communications consultant, Bath, England

Computer Science
K. Playford, B.Sc., postgraduate student, School of Mathematical Sciences, University of Bath, England

H. Litteck, B.Sc., GIMA, postgraduate student, School of Mathematical Sciences, University of Bath, England

Earth Science and Environmental Studies
P. Bunyard, M.A., co-editor of *The Ecologist*, Bodmin, England

R. J. G. Savage, B.Sc., Ph.D., Professor of Vertebrate Palaeontology, Department of Geology, University of Bristol, England

P. Hewitt, C.Eng., MIWEM, civil engineer and member of Institute of Water and Environmental Management

Energy
Dr. J. Crabb, B.Sc., Ph.D., Energy Studies Unit, University of Exeter, England

Health and Medicine
S. Mitchell, B.Sc., postgraduate student, Faculty of Medicine, University of Glasgow, Scotland

Physics
R. Draper, B.Sc., Research Officer, Physics Department, University of Bath, England

D. Parsons, B.Sc., Ph.D., H. H. Wills Physics Laboratory, University of Bristol, England

Space Technology
R. Keedwell, MITD, MCRAS, Principal Training officer, British Aerospace (Dynamics), Filton, England

Zoology
Philip Coffey, education officer, Jersey Wildlife Preservation Trust, England

C. West, scientific officer, Bristol Zoological Gardens, Bristol, England

Regional Consultants

Australia, New Zealand and the Pacific Islands
Brendan Schollum, senior lecturer in science education, Auckland College of Education, New Zealand

Indian subcontinent
Malti Kelkar, science teacher, author for the Indian School Science Curriculum; manager, Pune Bal Kalyan Sanstha, Recreational & Cultural Centre for Physically Handicapped Children, Pune, India

Southeast Asia
Lewis Sewell, M.Inst.CM, Cert. Ed. principal, formerly Clementi Town Primary School, Singapore

Middle East
Issa M. Jasim, Ph.D., Education (Elementary), Director of Educational Research Centre, Ministry of Education, Daeya, Kuwait

South Africa
Eddie Jansen, Chief Science Adviser, Department of Education & Training, Randburg, South Africa

North America
Winston Hoskins, Ph.D., Director of Science, Dallas Independent School District, Dallas, TX

UK/Europe
Elaine Davies, primary school head teacher and science adviser to Avon Educational Authority, Bath, England

STUDENT GUIDE

BRINE

Are you a scientist?

Chemists at work in a laboratory wear safety glasses to protect their eyes from the dangerous chemicals they are mixing.

Your answer to this question may be "no." But think again! In a way, we are all scientists. We are always asking questions and trying to find answers to things that we don't understand.

Just think of some of the problems you meet each day. Of course, they're not always very scientific. They could be as simple as how to change a bicycle tire or finding out where the rain comes from. But you can use scientific methods to solve most problems. By using a method of trial and error, you can try out ideas and solutions until you find the one that works best.

Science is all about solving problems. Your set of *Young Scientist* books will help you to focus on problems. Soon you will begin questioning everything around you. That is what real scientists do. They need to know how things happen.

Once you've decided what you need to know, you'll want to discover some answers. Your *Young Scientist* books will help you collect some information you need, either from experiments in your home or simply by observing the world around you.

This agricultural scientist is examining the growth of a spineless cactus.

Your *Young Scientist* set

Your *Young Scientist* set contains 10 books. Each of the first 9 helps you to explore two different areas of science and guide you as you carry out all kinds of fun activities. Look for these activities on the pages with a green border on the left-hand side. Important words are printed in dark, or bold, letters. Many of them are also explained in the glossary at the back of the book or the back of this volume. Look for a "Find out more" box at the top of a page. It will tell you where else to look in the same book for more information on the subject you are exploring.

Natural Science

Three books in the *Young Scientist* set explore our planet's resources, and the variety of living things—including ourselves.

1 Living world
Plants
Learn about the creatures and plants that live on our planet, from the tiniest cell to the largest animal. Find out about different kinds of plants and how they grow in different conditions around the world.

2 Human body
Conservation
Discover what your body is made of and how it works. Find out how we can use science to understand and protect our planet for the future.

3 Animals without backbones
Animals with backbones
Insects, corals, sponges, birds, and mammals are a few of the animals you can learn about in this book. Find out where and how they live, and learn to be a naturalist.

Physical and Earth Science

These three books examine the science and technology of our planet's main sources of energy.

4 Light and electricity
Magnetic power
Find out how electricity works and how to make your own electric circuits. Investigate the mysteries of light. Find out where it comes from and why we need it. Discover how magnetism produces energy and how this energy is used.

5 Atoms and molecules
Gases
Discover why substances are solids, liquids, or gases. Find out how they can change from one form to another, and how different substances react together. Find out about the many gases in our atmosphere—their similarities and their differences.

6 Planet Earth
Water
Explore the amazing planet on which we live—its mountains, seas, weather, and resources. Discover what water is made of, how we use it, and why we need it to survive.

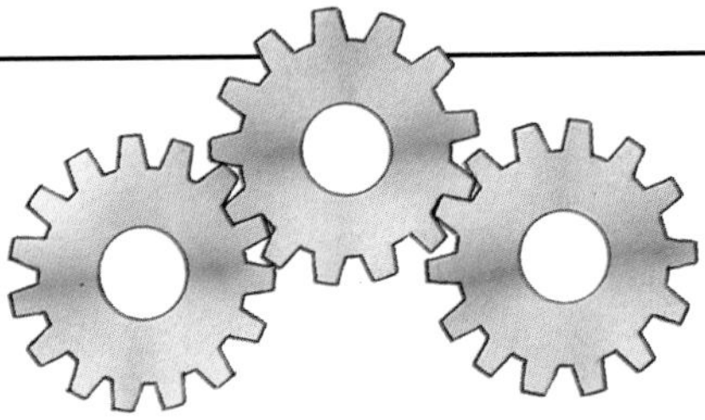

Applied Science and Technology

The following three books look in detail at how science and machines help make our lives easier.

7 Space technology
Computers
Read about the planets in our solar system and all the stars, including the sun. Discover the exciting world of space travel. See how computers work, and learn about everyday machines that use computers.

8 Communication
Energy
Discover how people send and store messages. Read about the different kinds of energy, including chemical energy, nuclear energy, and kinetic energy.

9 Construction
Machines
Explore the science of buildings, from the ancient pyramids to modern skyscrapers. Follow the development of machines through history. Investigate how levers, engines, motors, and turbines work.

10 Student guide/Index
Use this book to guide you through the *Young Scientist* set and to help you understand new scientific words and ideas.

What is science?

Science covers a broad field of knowledge dealing with facts that can be observed in the natural world or discovered by means of experiment.

Observation means using one's senses to look at something closely and to collect information, or **data**, about it. The children in the picture are making a scientific observation. They are observing a monarch butterfly and recording data in a notebook. They are also finding scientific data in a reference book on insects.

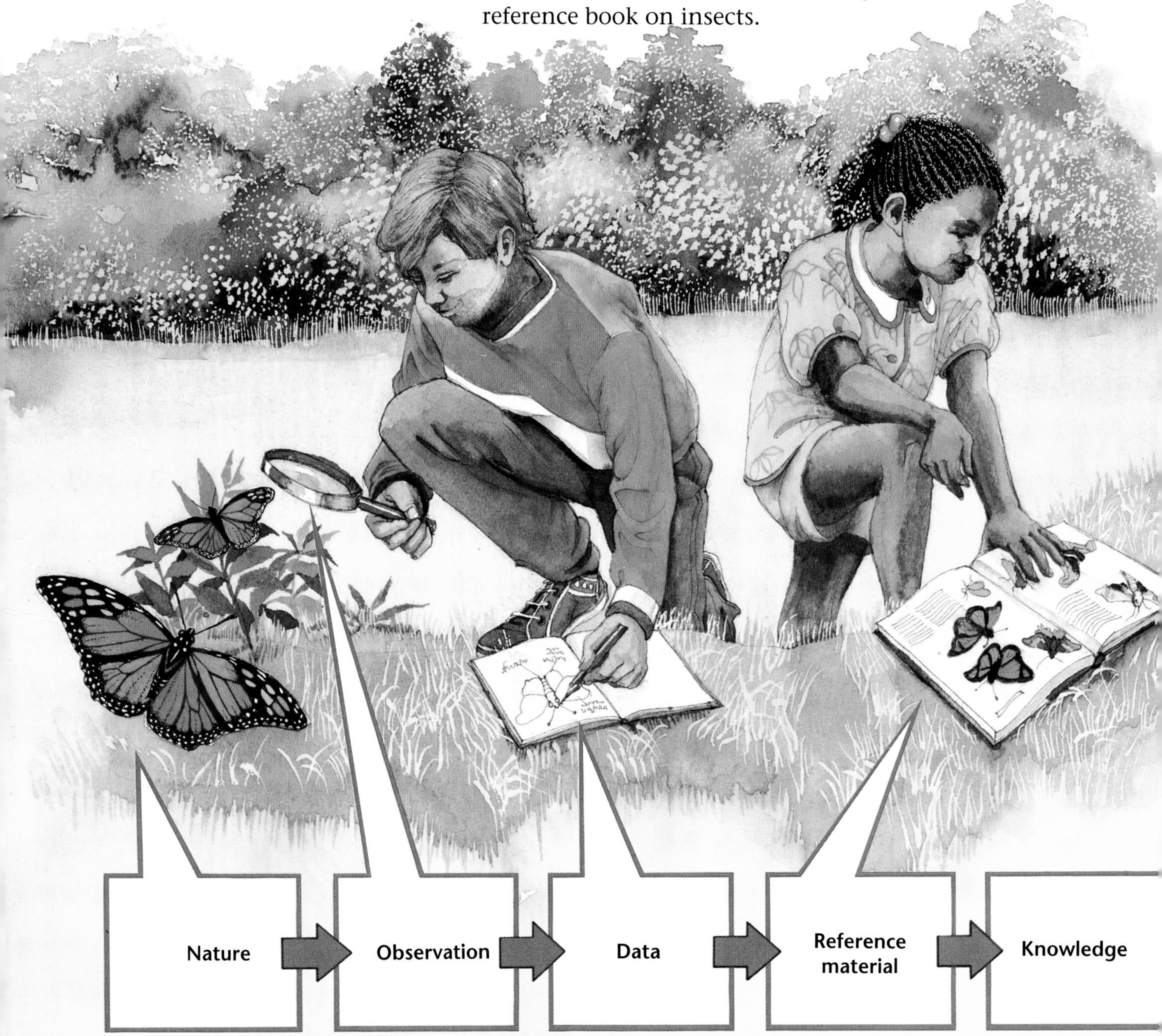

What is a fact?

Science describes objects and events, and then formulates ideas about them. The ideas are tested. If shown to be true, they become **facts.** Sometimes untested or untestable ideas are useful for further study. Such ideas that may or may not become facts are known as **theories.**

The diagram below follows the steps a scientist might take when trying to answer a question and arrive at a fact. The question asked in the diagram is: "Is the world round or flat?"

Identify the problem and ask a question.	Is the world round or flat? 
Decide on a theory.	The world is round. 
Design an experiment and then carry it out.	If the world is round and sailors in a ship set off in a straight line, they should end up back where they started. 
Collect data.	Sailors in a Spanish ship set sail to the west and after many months at sea returned to where they had started. 
Use the data.	When the sailors' route was charted onto a map, it was proved that they could sail around the world. 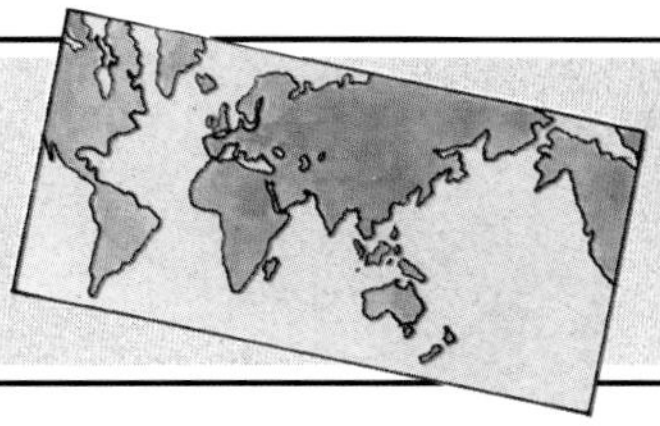
What is the fact?	The world is round. 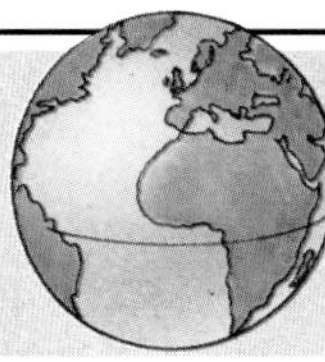

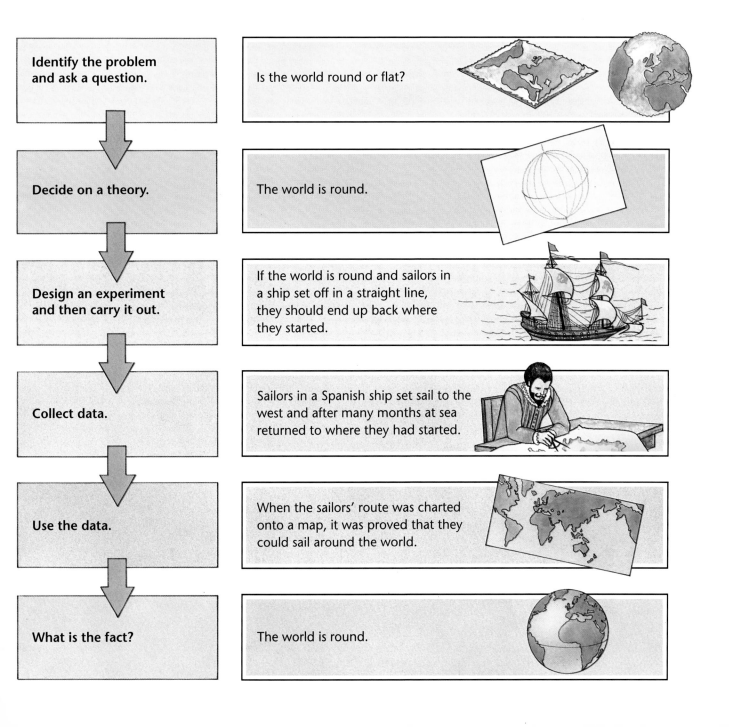

The natural world of science

Science is a subject that has many different parts. One part is the study of the world around us. It includes finding out about living plants and animals, from tiny cells and insects to giant trees and whales.

We can also learn about natural things that are not alive. These include gases in the air, rocks and minerals in the ground, and water in the seas and rivers. All these things form an important part of the planet Earth.

Science has helped us to know what our planet looked like millions—or even billions—of years ago. Scientists can use their research to look at fossils and find out about plant and animal species that were once alive but are now extinct.

This orchid belongs to a large family of plants, which contains more than 20,000 species. The smallest orchid is less than 0.4 inch (1 centimeter) high. The biggest can grow up to 100 feet (30 meters).

The Barbary ape is a wild monkey that lives on the Rock of Gibraltar, near Spain, and in parts of Morocco and Algeria in northern Africa.

Saturn is one of the planets in our solar system. Its rings are less of a mystery than they once were because of observations scientists have made, using telescopes, satellites, and computers.

Science in space

The natural world of science goes far beyond the limits of Earth. It takes us out into space! There we can study the other planets and stars that make up our universe. Observations made by scientists explain why we have night and day, how the moon affects the tides of the seas, and how the universe may have been formed.

This knowledge helps us understand the world we live in. It shows us how to make use of natural things, such as minerals and plants. Scientists have been able to send satellites into space and put people on the moon. Science even helps us see how the world might look in the future.

This scientist is wearing special germ-free, or sterile, clothing. He is placing a tray of blood samples in a modern unit where the samples are frozen and dried.

The artificial world of science

Scientists study the natural world to find out how it works. Then they can go a stage further. They can find out how to use things from the natural world to make new materials. These are the new chemicals, metals, and machines that help make our daily lives easier and more comfortable. The science of creating new things is called **technology.** Without it, we wouldn't have machines, plastics, or medicines. We would have to live on what we could find in the world around us, as cave people did thousands of years ago.

Old and new technology

You may think that technology is a modern way of using science. But people have been making tools and machines for many thousands of years. The wheel, for example, is about 5,000 years old. About 3,000 years ago, people were already making iron. They used fire, wood, and a special type of rock called pyrite, or iron ore. Over 250 years ago, scientists noticed that steam from boiling water tried to push its way out of the boiler. They soon realized that the force of this push could move a piston inside a cylinder. The piston could then be used to turn a wheel. This was how steam engines were invented. They were made from iron and had the same power as hundreds of horses.

Technology is improving all the time. We now have machines to help us do many different jobs, from brushing our teeth to traveling around the world. But everything in our artificial world is the result of making science work for us.

Computer technology is changing the way we live. Computers can help us to work out difficult calculations quickly or learn about the world around us—at the touch of a button.

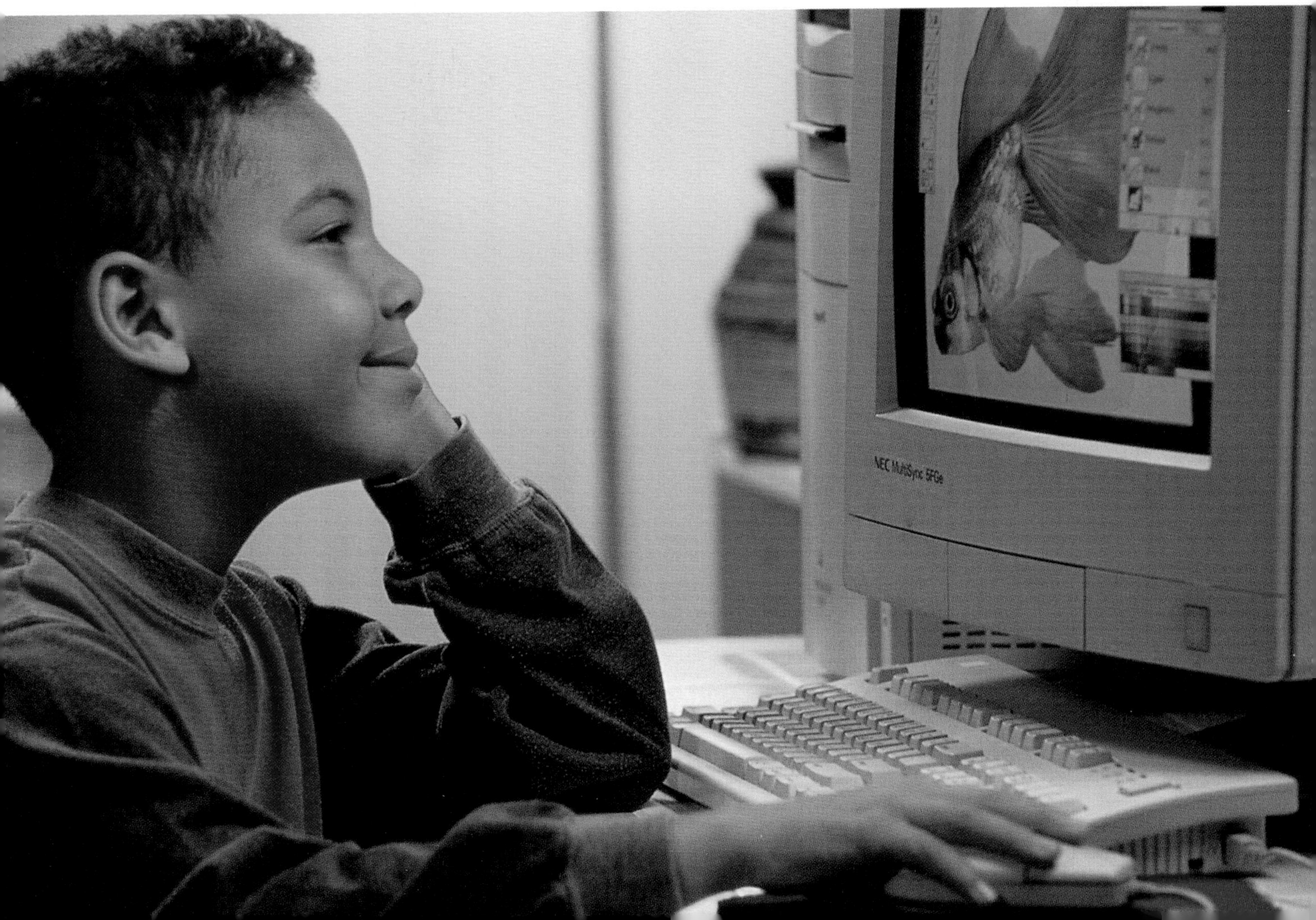

The hidden world of science

Science helps us to learn about things that we can't even see. The smallest objects that your eyes can see are about 1/100 of an inch (0.25 of a millimeter) across. The hidden world of science is filled with tiny animals, bacteria, and nonliving things that are far smaller than this. In order to look at these tiny things and study them, scientists have to make them appear bigger. We call this **magnifying.**

To magnify what cannot be seen, scientists need either a hand lens or a microscope. There are many different kinds of lenses and microscopes. Some can magnify things more than others. It all depends on how big we want something to appear. A hand lens, for example, can make something look 10 times bigger than it really is. An electron microscope can magnify something up to 1 million times!

Scientists use powerful electron microscopes to investigate tiny things, such as viruses, bacteria, and atoms.

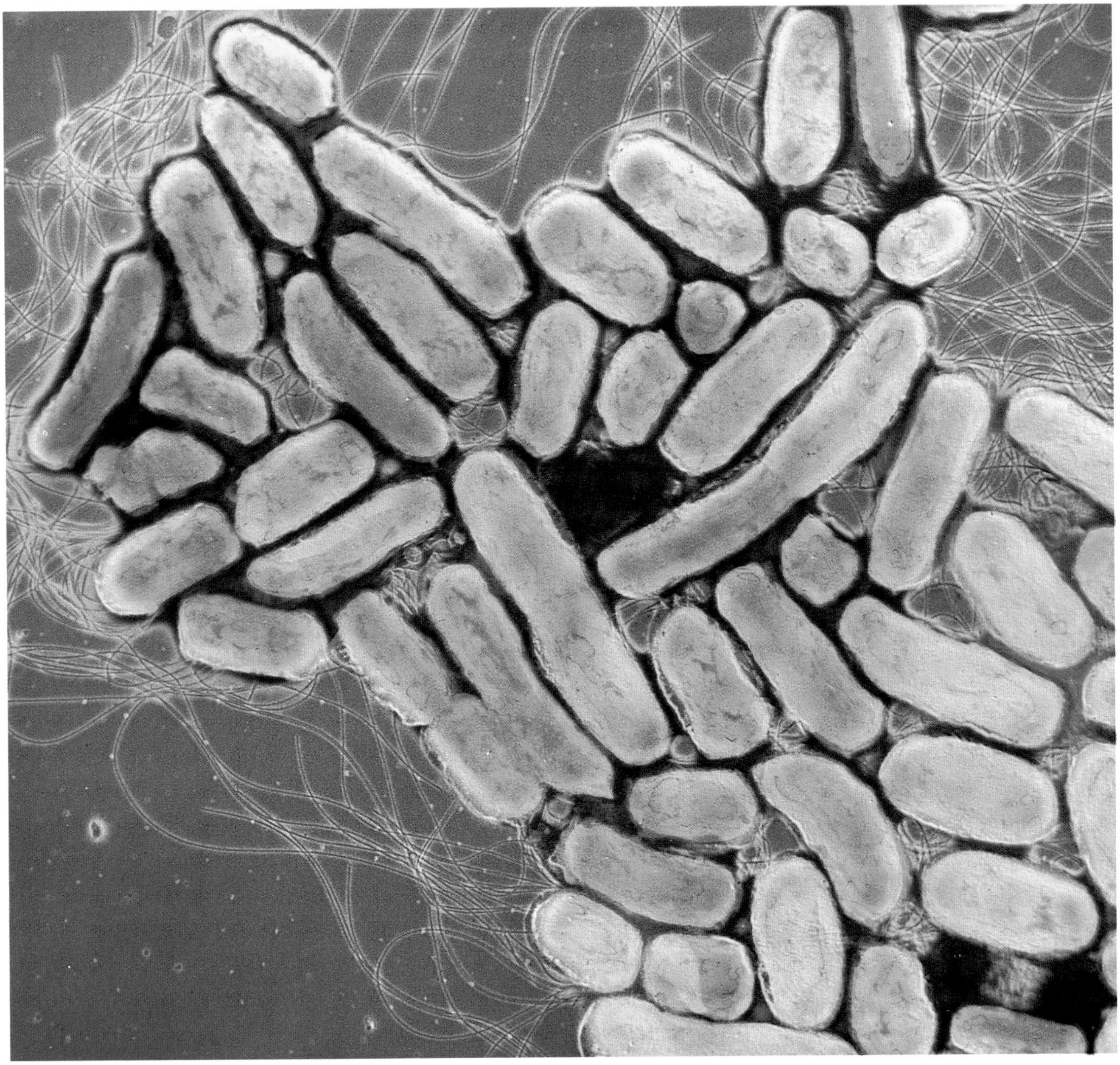

This group, or colony, of bacteria has been photographed with an electron microscope.

Studying the invisible

Some things, such as atoms and molecules, are so tiny that they cannot be seen with ordinary microscopes. Instead scientists photograph them with electron microscopes. These pictures are magnified and recorded by a special camera.

We cannot see many gases, either. But by collecting them and carrying out different experiments, scientists can tell us many things about gases. In the world of science, we don't always need to see something to be able to describe it.

The work of a scientist

Science has become an important area of learning. It is such a large subject that to study all of it would be impossible. So scientists concentrate on the area of science that interests them most. They **specialize** in one particular area, such as biology, chemistry, or physics.

Biology is one of the three main areas of science. **Chemistry** and **physics** are the other two. But even these categories can be too general. To learn about things in detail, scientists must specialize even further. For example, a biologist may study only plants. This type of biologist is called a **botanist.** A biologist who studies only animals is called a **zoologist.** The diagram below shows some of the many different areas of science that scientists can study.

The biologist

A biologist studies what living things are, what they are made of and how they behave.

The botanist

Botanists study how plants and fungi live and grow. They explore ways of using plants for food or for medicines.

The chemist

A chemist studies what substances are made of and how they behave when mixed together.

The geologist

Geologists study substances in Earth, how Earth was formed and how it changes.

The physicist

A physicist studies matter and how it is affected by sources of energy, such as electricity.

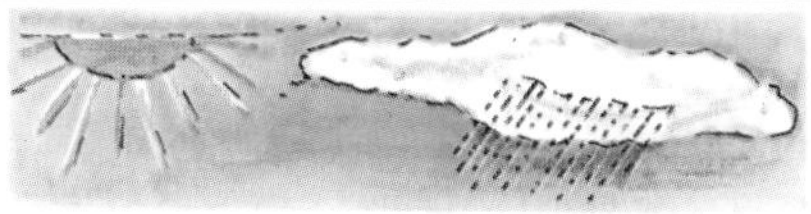

The meteorologist

Meteorologists look at Earth's atmosphere and measure the changes that produce our weather.

Research teams

The job of many scientists is to find out more about their specialized area. In this way, they hope to add to the knowledge we already have. They are called **research scientists.** They work with special equipment in laboratories, outdoors, and even in space.Scientists may work in teams. Each member of a team may specialize in a different area. For example, a pharmacist may be trying to discover a new medicine. The team might have a botanist, who knows which plants can be used to manufacture drugs. An **X-ray crystallographer** can tell how the atoms in a drug are arranged. A **biochemist** might work with physicians to learn how new medicines will affect human bodies.

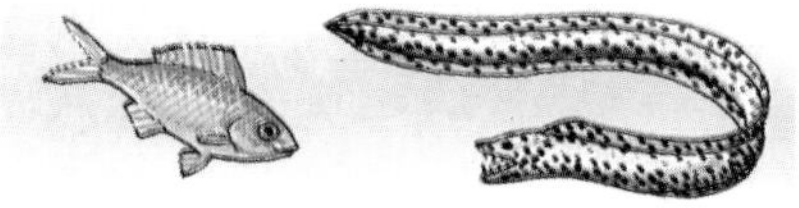

The marine biologist

Marine biologists study plants and animals in the sea, from huge whales to tiny diatoms.

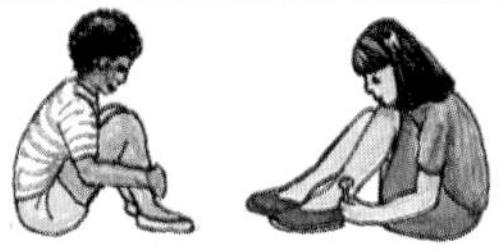

The human biologist

Human biologists study how the human body works, what can go wrong with it and how it can be cured.

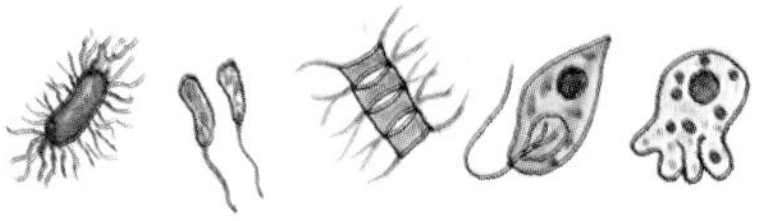

The microbiologist

Microbiologists study tiny creatures, such as algae and bacteria, which can only be seen through a microscope.

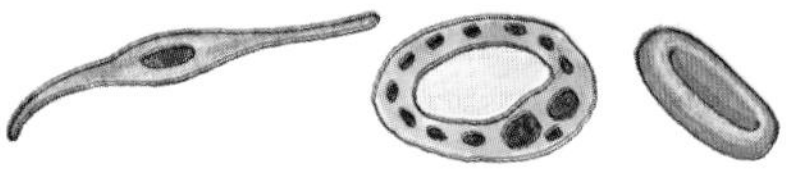

The biochemist

Biochemists find out about the chemical processes that make all living things work.

The pharmacist

Pharmacists make drugs and medicines to treat diseases.

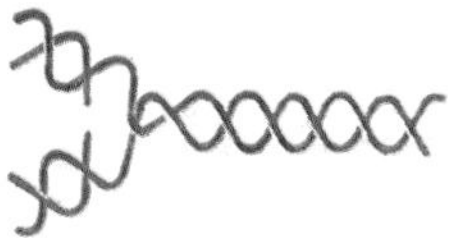

The physical chemist

Physical chemists study the atoms and molecules that make up matter. They make models like this one.

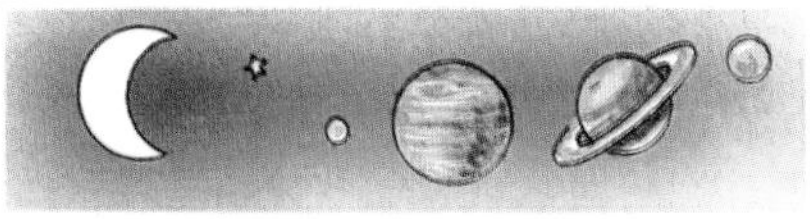

The astronomer

Astronomers study everything in the universe, like stars and planets. They try to discover how parts of the universe work.

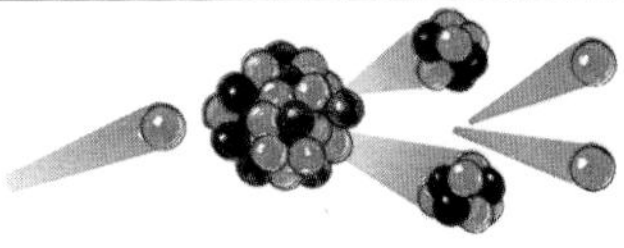

The nuclear physicist

Nuclear physicists study the behavior of tiny particles inside atoms.

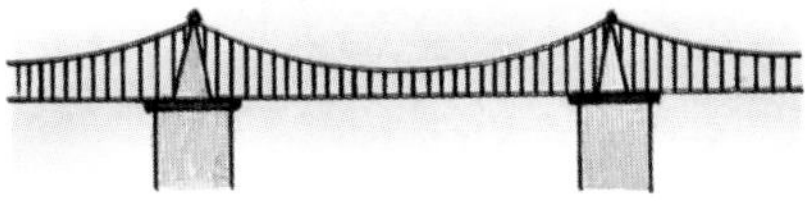

The civil engineer

Civil engineers plan and supervise the building of large construction projects, such as bridges and tunnels.

Becoming a young scientist

In the set of *Young Scientist* books, you will find many new words. Soon you will build up quite a large store of words. Scientists use special names for every single thing that makes up the world in which we live. This way, they can tell us about the discoveries they make. For example, scientists have names for every part of the human body. Using a name for each part, they are able to efficiently describe how and why we become ill. Scientists work together and share their common knowledge in order to make discoveries that improve medicines and procedures. Imagine if all the scientists in history had made their discoveries but didn't have the words to tell us about them!

Learning new words is an important part of being a scientist. The glossaries in each book will help you understand the language of science. Keep them close at hand, so you can easily look up words you don't understand.

Be organized!

As you are carrying out an experiment or an activity, you should record your results. Your *Young Scientist* books will show you different ways of keeping records. If you keep a clear and accurate record of your work, you will be able to use what you have learned. You will see how pieces of scientific information fit together. You can then use what you have learned to understand other data.

Your notebook is only one place where you need to be tidy and orderly. Try to organize your reading and even your thinking. Concentrate on one experiment at a time. You will find this much easier, safer, and more fun than if you try to understand a hundred different things at once!

These children are finding out how water travels through tiny tubes inside a plant's stem. They are making a rainbow salad, using water, celery stalks, and food coloring.

A place to work

Many scientists work in specially prepared rooms called **laboratories.** These rooms are filled with instruments and materials that scientists need to carry out their experiments. Have you ever been inside a laboratory? Perhaps you have one at school. At home, you can do some scientific experiments at your kitchen sink or at a table.

What do you need?

You will need plenty of clear space, so the most important thing is a large table or surface where you can work. For many experiments, you will have to use water. A sink is useful for cleaning your equipment after you have used it. Try to find a cupboard or a large space where you can store your equipment neatly and safely. This will help you to put everything away and set up your laboratory again quickly.

Setting up

Once you've found a place to do your laboratory activities, you can set it up. It may be a kitchen or utility room, so remember not to get in the way or make a mess. First of all, cover your work surface with plenty of newspaper. This will protect the surface and make cleaning up quick and easy. Make sure that you have a pencil and notebook beside you, so that you can record all your findings and observations as you go along. By looking in the *Young Scientist* book from which you have chosen to work, you will know what to collect. The equipment and materials can then be arranged on your work surface, and you're ready to begin an experiment!

Your work surface

Here is one way of dividing up your work surface. Make separate areas for doing an experiment, for writing about it, and for storing the materials you will need.

storage area
work area
writing area

Clearing up

Clear everything away neatly at the end of each activity or experiment. This will make it easy to set up quickly the next time you do a project. As you work your way through the books of your *Young Scientist* set, your collection of equipment, materials and finished objects will grow bigger and bigger. So make sure you have plenty of containers and a large box or tray where you can store them.

Start collecting empty boxes for keeping paper, plastic, and cardboard. Pots are useful for storing paper clips, thumbtacks, nails, and other small fasteners. If you are keeping liquids or solids that spill easily, make sure the container has a tight-fitting lid. Remember to label every container before you put it away. This will help you to find what you need the next time you set up your work area.

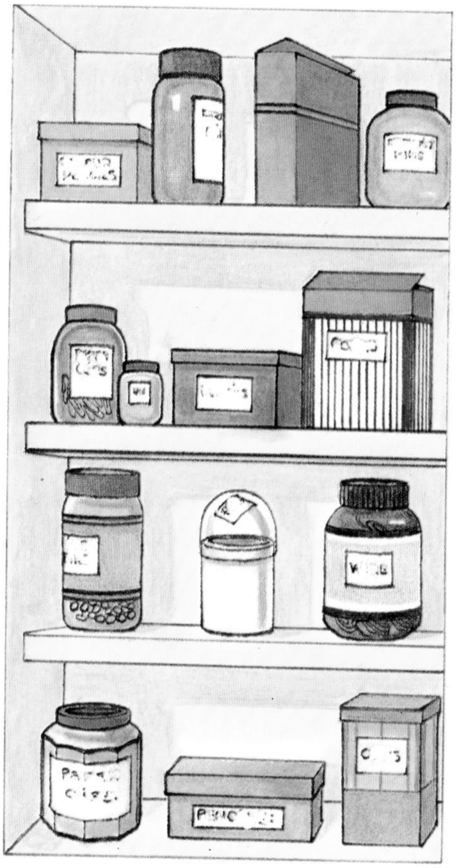

This girl is making a magnetic puppet theater. She is well prepared.

Keeping a record of your work

Have you ever done a jigsaw puzzle? Science is like a jigsaw puzzle. Every experiment and everything you read is like a small piece of knowledge. These pieces usually fit together to build up an understanding of science. Piece by piece, knowledge builds on other knowledge.

You will need to keep a record of all the experiments you do and their results. In this way, you can build up your own science jigsaw puzzle. You can keep your own science file, where you make notes about your laboratory experiments and record any other scientific data you have gathered. Your file can include charts, drawings, and tables to help you remember anything you think is interesting and important.

This is one suggestion for a page describing a wood louse. You might want to do it differently.

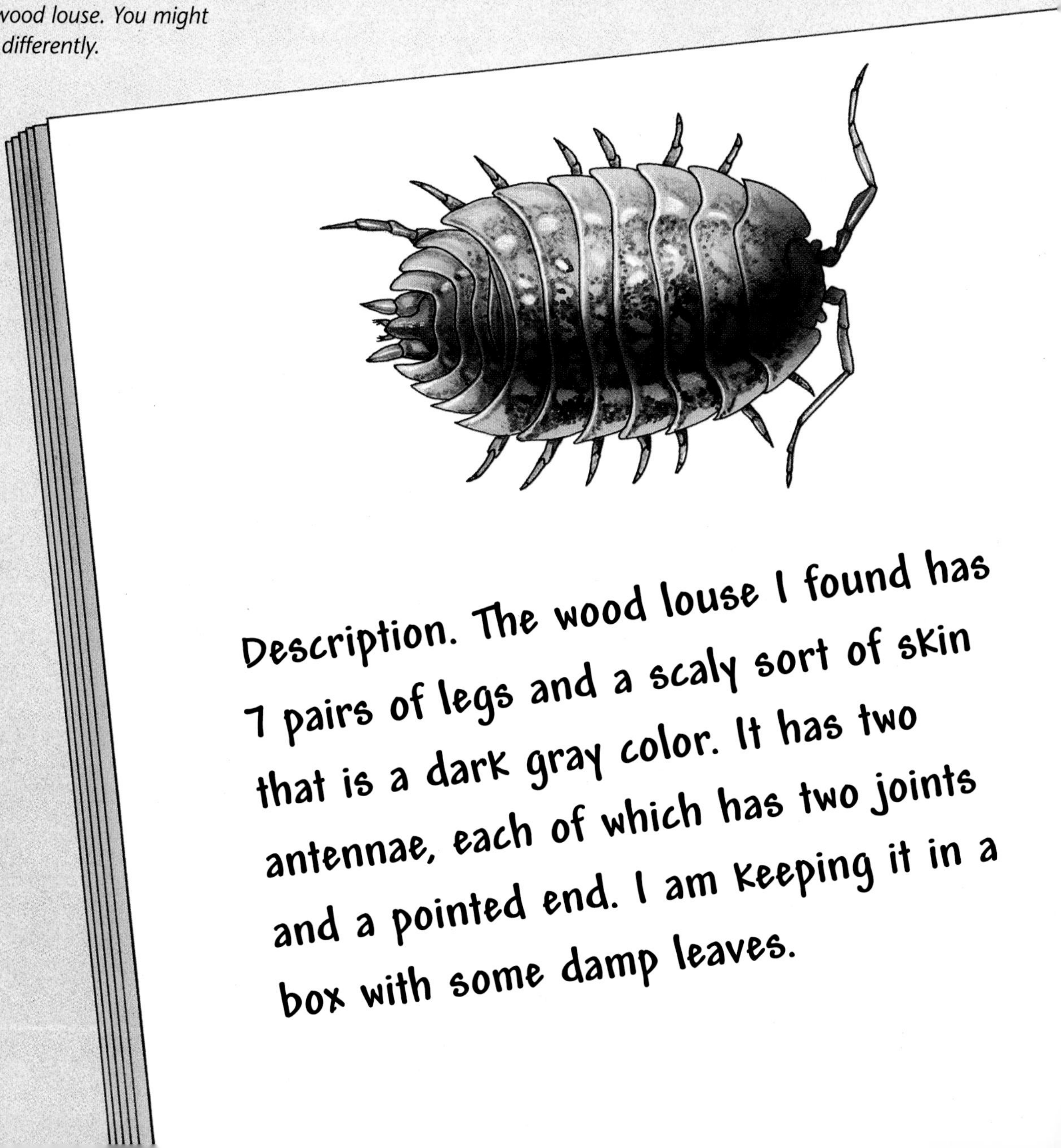

Description. The wood louse I found has
7 pairs of legs and a scaly sort of skin
that is a dark gray color. It has two
antennae, each of which has two joints
and a pointed end. I am keeping it in a
box with some damp leaves.

Recording information

Your *Young Scientist* books suggest what you should record and how you can best record data in a clear and interesting way. But with practice, you will soon want to add ideas of your own. Remember that you may need to use your notes and drawings again later, so make sure they are neat and clear.

Date: May 5, 2001

Book: Invertebrates,
Animals without backbones.

Name of the invertebrate—wood louse

Weather—damp and cloudy.

Habitat—I found it underneath a piece of dead wood lying in the corner of the park.

size—.6 inch (15 mm) and .3 inch (7 mm) wide.

Movement—It was standing still, feeling the wood with its antennae. When I disturbed it, it rolled up into a ball.

Using equipment

Making things is a fun way to find out how everyday machines and equipment work. Your *Young Scientist* books will ask you to make many different things, using all kinds of materials and equipment.

Following is a list of some of the pieces of equipment you will need as you work through the books. Remember that some pieces of equipment could hurt you if you don't use them properly. Always make sure you hold cutting tools correctly so that they cannot slip. Keep your fingers well out of the way when you are cutting, hammering, or sawing. If you think you could hurt yourself, stop and ask an adult for help.

Which battery can you use?

In several of your *Young Scientist* books, you will find experiments that need batteries. In these experiments, the **"You will need"** section recommends you use either a 1.5-volt ("D") or a 6-volt battery.

You will find that batteries come in various shapes and sizes. It doesn't matter what a battery looks like. It may or may not look like one pictured here.

The important thing to remember is to get the voltage right. Try to find a battery with a voltage as near as possible to 1.5 volts or 6 volts. For example, in some countries, there may also be 4.5-volt batteries available. The experiments will also work with these batteries. **Remember to never use a battery that produces more than 6 volts.**

If you can only find 1.5-volt batteries, buy four and put them together in the way shown below. Two 1.5-volt batteries joined together are the same as a 3-volt battery. Four 1.5-volt batteries are the same as a 6-volt battery.

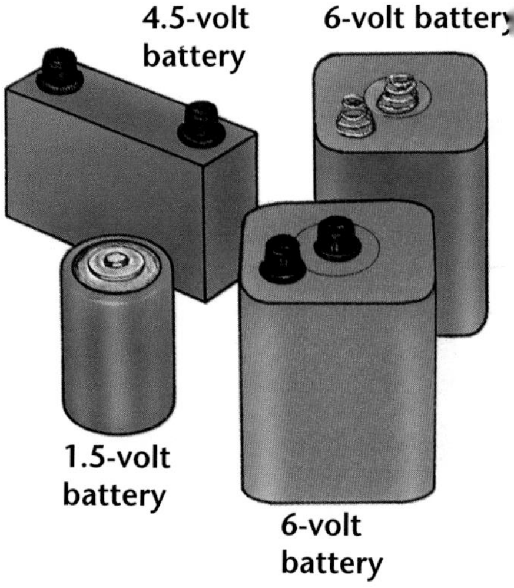

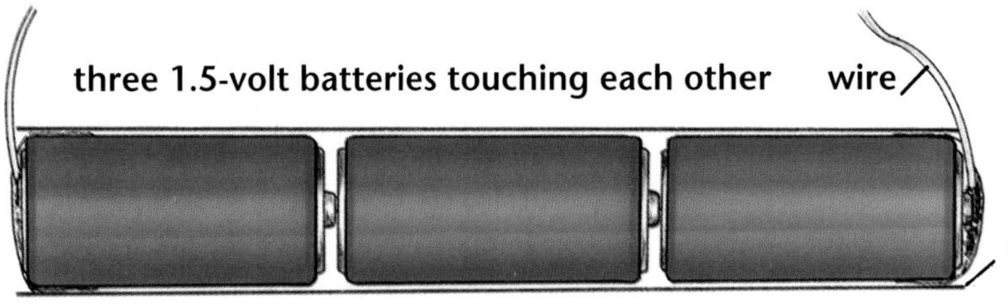

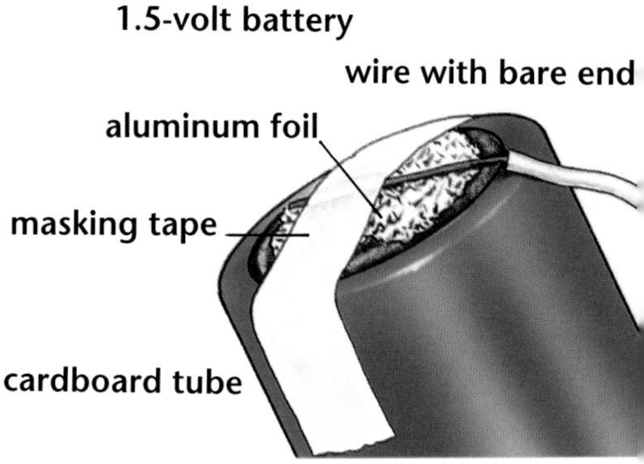

Scissors

Scissors with blades about 4 inches (10 centimeters) long are useful for cutting paper and thin cardboard. Choose a pair with blunt ends and remember to carry them safely clenched downward in your fist.

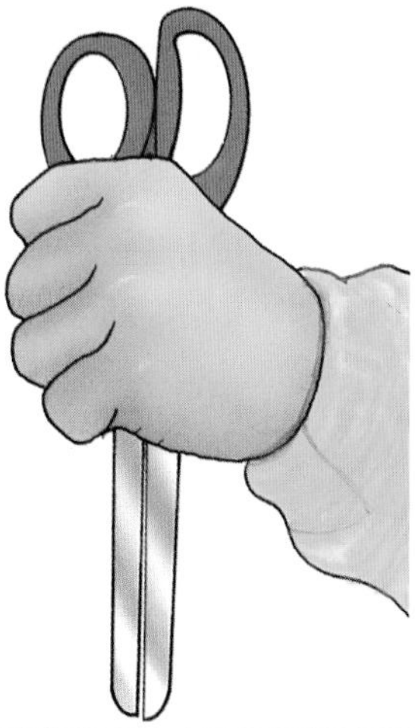

Hammers

Hold a nail and tap it gently about ⅛ of an inch (3 millimeters) into a piece of wood. Then move your fingers out of the way and bang the nail in. Nailing together two pieces of wood is quicker than gluing them. Use a hammer with a steel head.

Saws

This saw has hundreds of tiny sharp teeth to cut through wood. If the wood is thick and difficult to cut, ask an adult to help you.

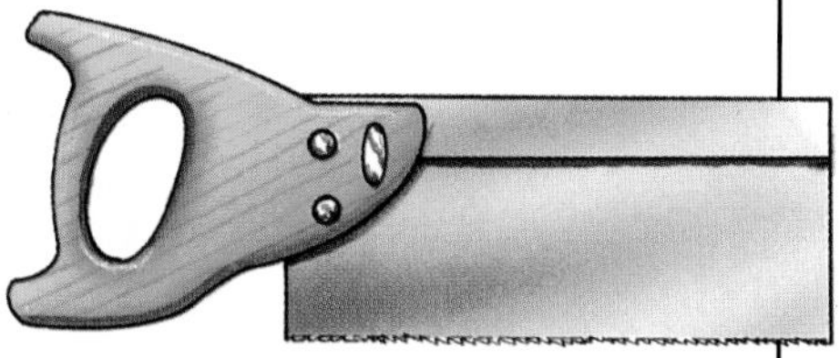

Wire cutters

This tool is a pair of wire cutters. You can use it to cut electric wire and to strip off the plastic insulation.

Wood

Newspaper can protect your table from the mess caused by glue and water. But if you are cutting, banging, and sawing, use a large plank of wood to protect the work surface.

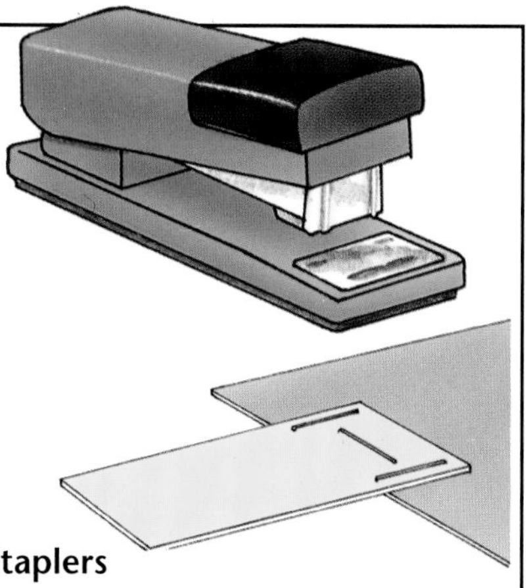

Staplers

A small stapler is very useful for quickly joining together pieces of paper or thin cardboard.

Screwdrivers

Screws usually have straight slots or cross-shaped slots. Each type of screw needs the right sort of screwdriver to fit.

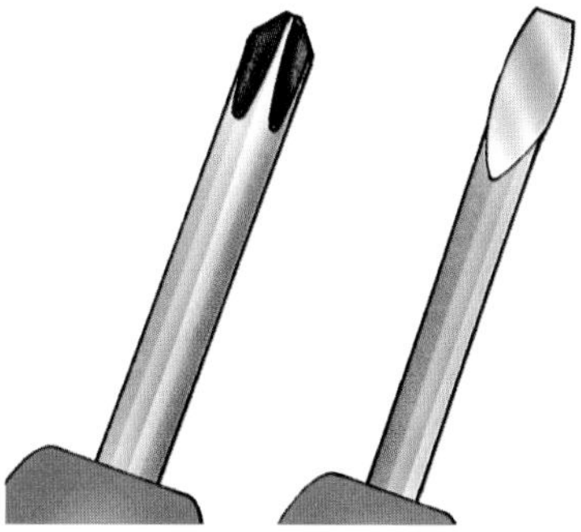

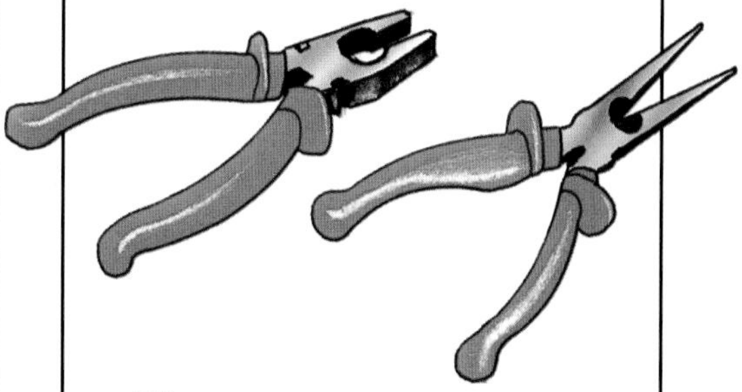

Pliers

Pliers can grip things more tightly than your fingers can. Some pairs of pliers have long pointed ends for holding things in awkward places.

Finding materials

In your *Young Scientist* books, you will find a lot of activities that will help you learn by doing, making, and having fun. At the beginning of each activity, you will see the words "**You will need,**" followed by a list of materials and equipment. Try to collect everything together on your work surface before you begin.

Some materials may be expensive to buy. But if you look around, you will be surprised to find how many of these materials people throw away. If you have somewhere to store them all, you could start a collection of materials now. That way you won't have to spend time searching around for them when you need them.

Materials you will need

Here are some suggestions for materials to use in your activities and experiments.

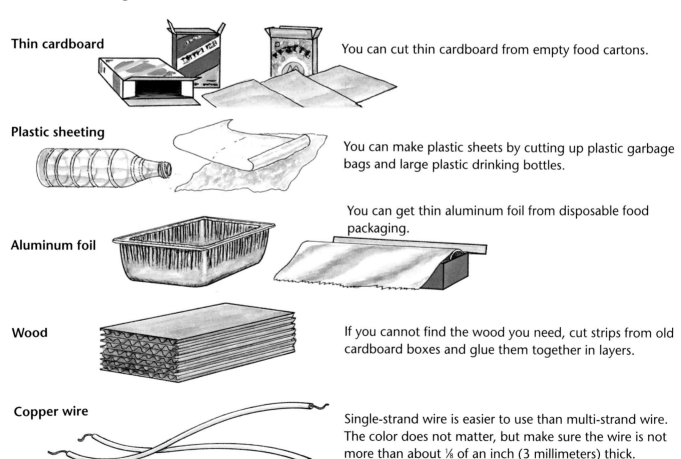

Thin cardboard

You can cut thin cardboard from empty food cartons.

Plastic sheeting

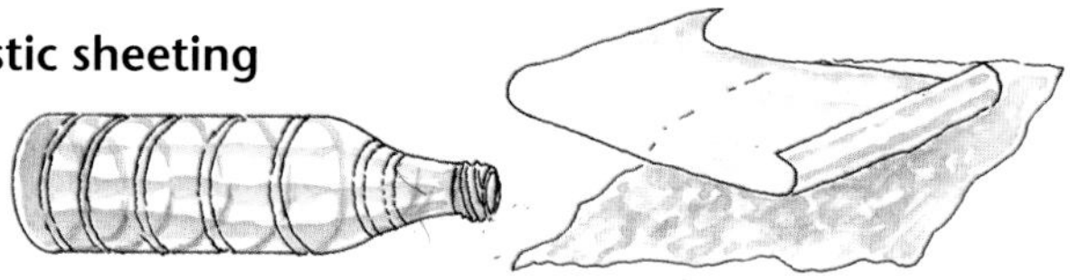

You can make plastic sheets by cutting up plastic garbage bags and large plastic drinking bottles.

Aluminum foil

You can get thin aluminum foil from disposable food packaging.

Wood

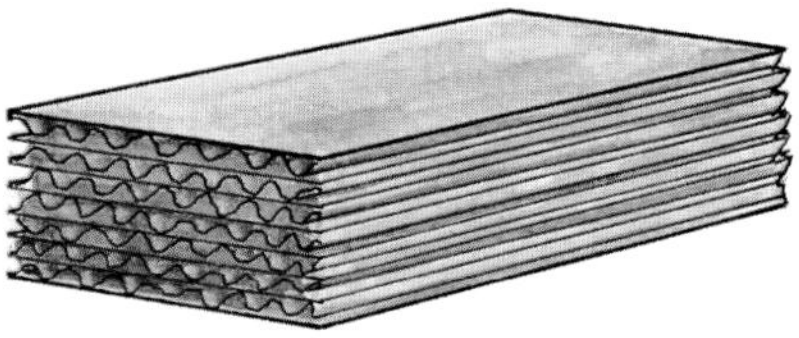

If you cannot find the wood you need, cut strips from old cardboard boxes and glue them together in layers.

Copper wire

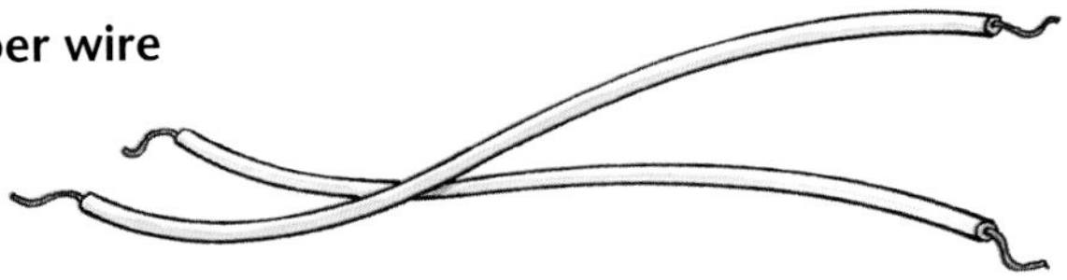

Single-strand wire is easier to use than multi-strand wire. The color does not matter, but make sure the wire is not more than about ⅛ of an inch (3 millimeters) thick.

Tape

Adhesive tape and masking tape quickly fasten cardboard and paper.

Modeling clay

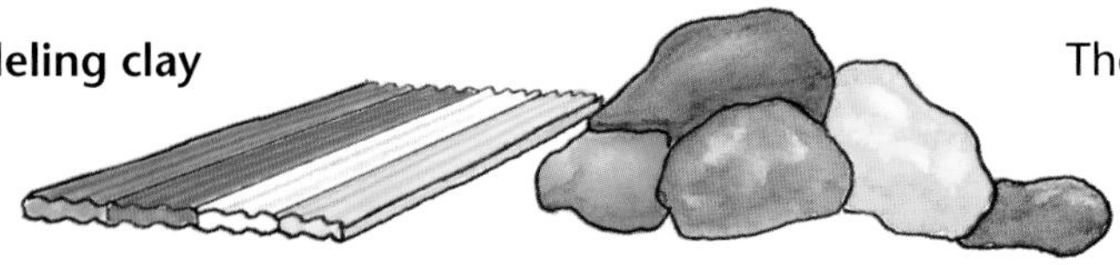

There are many different kinds of modeling clay.

Thumbtacks

You will sometimes need thumbtacks. Check if they are made of steel by trying to pick them up with a magnet.

Nails

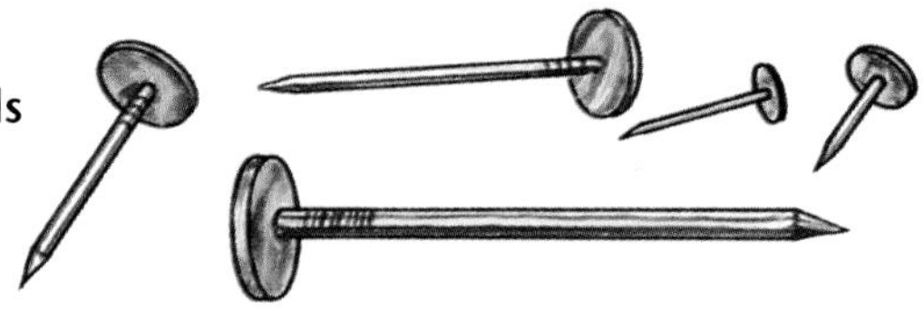

Choose nails that are the right length for the wood you are nailing.

Paper clips

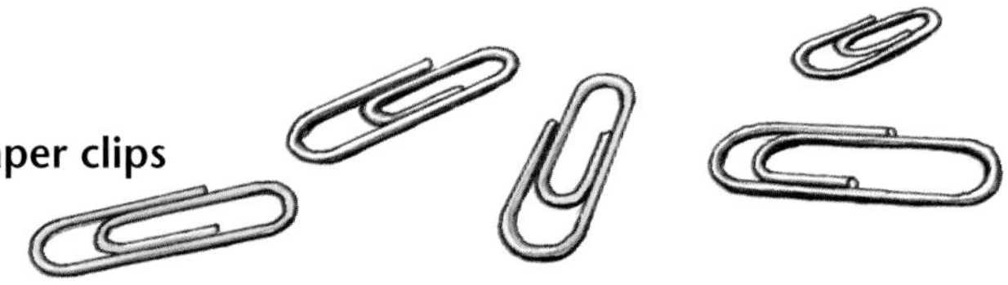

You will sometimes need steel paper clips. Check if they are steel by trying to pick them up with a magnet.

Paper fasteners

You can turn around pieces of paper when they are held together with this sort of fastener.

Bulbs

1.5-volt bulb

6-volt bulb

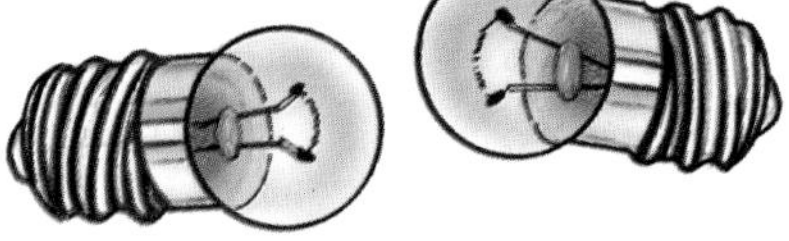

Choose small light bulbs that match the voltage of your battery.

Bulb holders

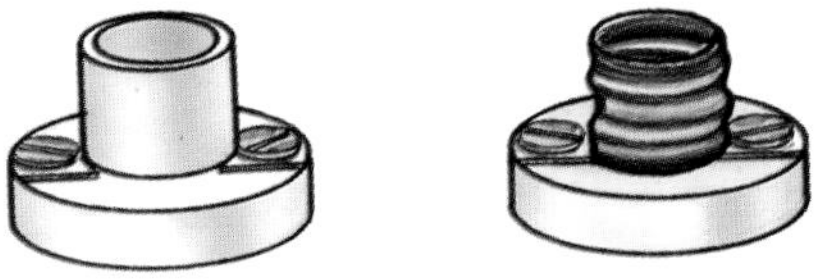

These bulb holders help you to attach wires to small light bulbs in an electric circuit.

Glue

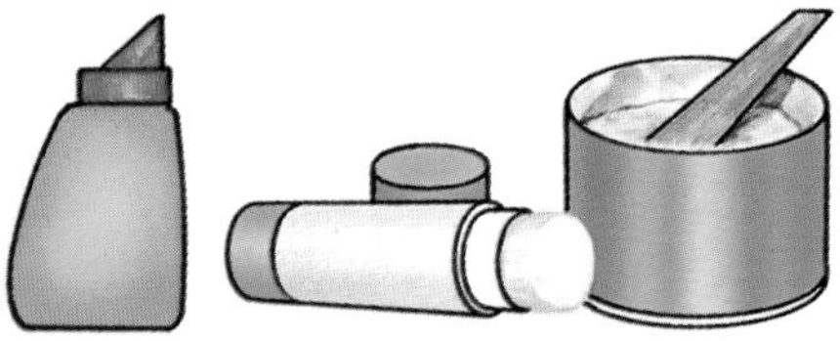

Are you joining wood or paper or plastic? Make sure you choose the right sort of glue. Always follow the instructions on the container.

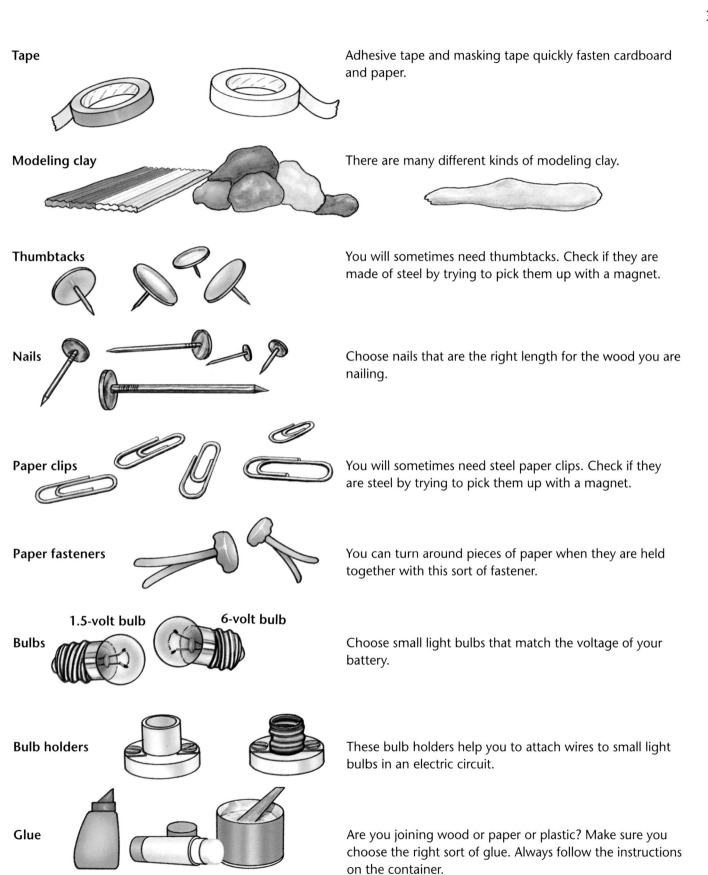

Learning to measure

Scientists spend a lot of time measuring things. As you work through your *Young Scientist* books, you will have to measure things, too. There are three main things to measure. These are **mass, distance**, and **time.** We measure each of these in amounts called **units.**

How big is a pound?

When you measure the **mass** of something, you find out how much matter it contains. The unit of mass that scientists generally use is a **pound** (0.45 kilogram). Find a bag of sugar that is marked 16 ounces, or 1 lb. This means that the mass of the sugar is one pound. A pound (0.45 kilogram) is usually written as 1 lb (0.45 kg) for short.

Don't confuse **mass** and **weight.** Your mass always stays the same, but weight changes with the force of gravity.

Perhaps your mass is about 66 pounds (30 kilograms). On Earth, gravity pulls down on mass, so we say that your weight is 66 pounds (30 kilograms), too. On the moon, gravity is only one-sixth as strong as on Earth. Your mass is still 66 pounds (30 kilograms) but your weight would be one-sixth of this. You would only weigh 11 pounds (5 kilograms).

You weigh 66 lbs (30 kg) on Earth.
You weigh 11 lbs (5 kg) on the moon.

How long is a foot?

When you measure the **distance** between two things, you find out how far apart they are. The unit of distance that scientists generally use is a **foot** (0.3 meter). This is shortened to ft (m).

Stretch your arms out wide. The distance between your fingertips is about 3 feet (1 meter).

How long is a second?

When you measure **time**, you find out how long it takes for something to happen. The unit of time that scientists generally use is called a **second.** This is shortened to 1 sec.

Hang a weight from the end of a piece of string 1 foot (0.3 meter) long. Hold the other end of the string in your left hand. With your right hand, lift the weight keeping the string straight, and then let it swing. The weight will take one second to swing back to its original position.

The second hand on a clock takes about this long to move one second.

Bigger and smaller units

This girl is trying to measure her thumbnail with a ruler.

You do not measure your age in seconds or the width of your thumbnail in feet. Seconds are too small and feet are too big for these jobs. Pounds are also too big if you want to measure the mass of a fly. Scientists have invented bigger and smaller units based on these three main units, so that we can measure anything.

There are 12 inches in 1 foot, and 3 feet in 1 yard (12 in = 1 ft).
There are 1,000 millimeters in 1 meter (1,000 mm = 1 m).
There are 100 centimeters in 1 meter (100 cm = 1 m).
There are 5,280 feet in one mile (5,280 ft = 1 mi).
There are 1,000 meters in 1 kilometer (1,000 m = 1 km).

There are 16 ounces in 1 pound (16 oz = 1 lb).
There are 1,000 grams in 1 kilogram (1,000 g = 1 kg).
There are 2,000 pounds in 1 short ton (2,000 lb = 1 ton).
There are 1,000 kilograms in 1 metric ton (1,000 kg = 1 t).

There are 60 seconds in one minute (60 sec = 1 min).
There are 60 minutes in one hour (60 min = 1 hr).

Shorter names
The names of units can be shortened so that they are easier to write. We shorten
one foot to 1 ft,
one meter to 1 m,
one ounce to 1 oz,
one kilogram to 1 kg,
one second to 1 sec.

Measuring in units

You will often use the three main units to measure things. But the units can tell you much more than just mass, distance or time. Feet help us to measure area and volume. Pounds help us to find out the density of an object. Feet and seconds help us to work out the speed of an object.

Measuring area

How much space does a football field take up? We measure the **area** to find out. The main unit of area is the **square foot.** Imagine a square with sides one foot long. This is a square foot. One square foot can be written as **1 sq ft.** A smaller unit of area is the square inch, **sq in.** In the metric system, a square meter is $\mathbf{m^2}$, a square centimeter $\mathbf{cm^2}$, and a square millimeter $\mathbf{mm^2}$.

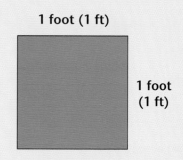

1 foot (1 ft)

1 foot (1 ft)

Take a square with sides one foot long. You could fit 57,600 of these squares onto a football field. So we say that a football field has an area of 57,600 square feet, or 57,600 sq ft. The metric equivalent is 5,351 m^2.

What is the area of the cover of a *Young Scientist* book? The height of the cover is about 11 inches (28 centimeters) and the width is about 9 inches (23 centimeters).

9 in (23 cm)

11 in (28 cm)

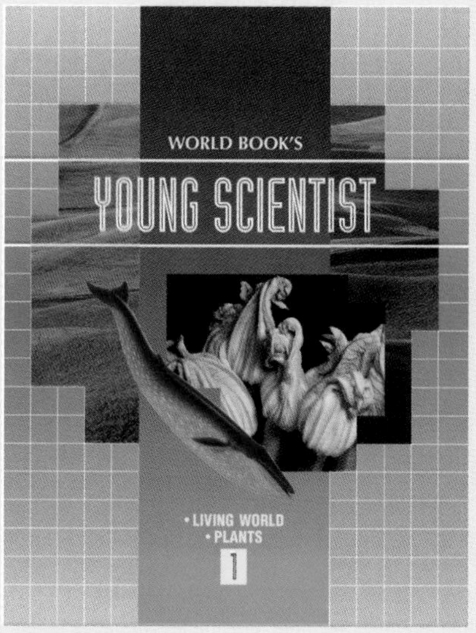

The area is 11 in × 9 in (28 cm × 23 cm), which equals 99 square inches (644 square centimeters), 11 in × 9 in = 99 sq in (28 cm × 23 cm = 644 cm^2).

What is volume?

How much space is there inside your room? We measure the **volume** to find out. The main unit of volume is the **cubic foot.** Imagine a cube with sides one foot long. This is a cubic foot. One cubic foot can be written as **1 cu ft.** Other units of volume are the cubic inch **(cu in)**, the cubic yard **(cu yd)** and the quart **(qt)**. In the metric system, a cubic meter is $\mathbf{m^3}$, a cubic centimeter $\mathbf{cm^3}$, and a liter **L**.

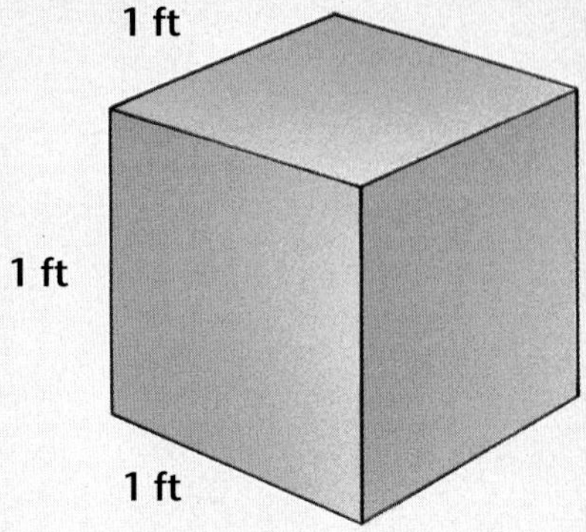

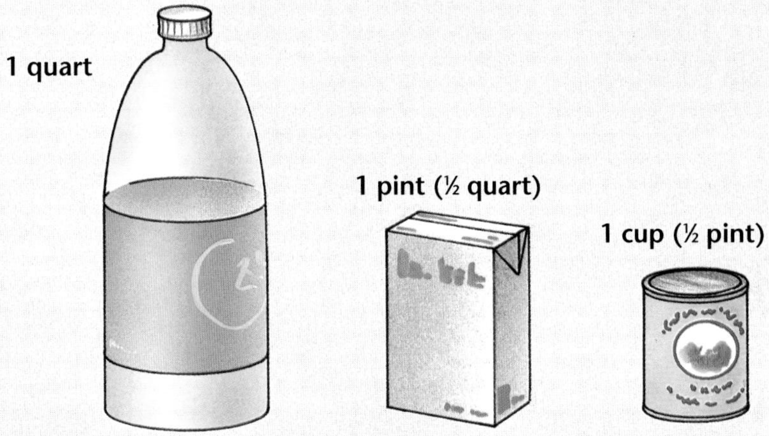

We can say how much liquid there is in a container by measuring its volume. The volume of this bottle is 1 quart (0.95 liter). There are 2 pints in a quart, and 2 cups in a pint.

What is density?

Suppose you want to compare two different substances, such as water and lead. People often say that lead is much heavier than water. But a lake full of water is much heavier than a small block of lead. These people have forgotten to say how much water and how much lead they are comparing.

To compare two substances properly, you must compare the same volume of each. Scientists compare substances by measuring their **density.** Density is a measure of the mass of one cubic centimeter of a substance. The metric system, as well as the inch/pound system, are used to measure density.

The mass of one cubic centimeter of lead is 11.35 grams. The mass of one cubic centimeter of water is 1 gram. So we can say that the density of lead is 11.35 grams per cubic centimeter (11.35 g/cm^3), and the density of water is 1 gram per cubic centimeter (1 g/cm^3).

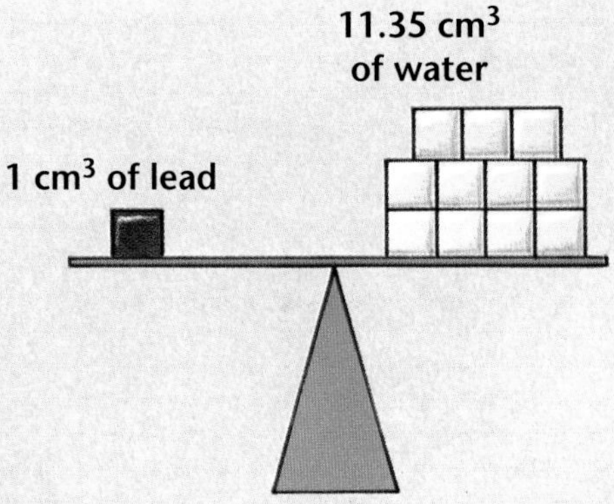

Lead is more dense than water. One cubic centimeter of lead equals 11.35 cubic centimeters of water.

Equipment for measuring

Now that you have learned about the different units of measurement, you need to find out what measuring equipment you can use. The equipment you choose will depend on what you have at home or can make yourself. You must also think about the size of what you are measuring and how accurate your measurements need to be. For example, if you were measuring the distance from your house to your school, you wouldn't use a ruler. The distance would be too large and the units of measurement on your ruler would be too small. How could you make this measurement?

Measuring time

What time is it? How old are you? When does the film start? The answers to all these questions are measures of time that we use every day. We rarely need to use seconds. But in science, things often happen very quickly and the answers to scientific questions must be exact. For scientific experiments and activities, you will need to have a second hand on your clock or watch. Scientists may use even smaller units called milliseconds. There are 1,000 milliseconds in one second!

Ordinary clocks and watches measure hours, minutes, and seconds. You can stop and start some digital watches to see how long something has taken.

Measuring mass

When scientists measure mass, they need to be very accurate. The tiniest difference of mass might make an important difference to their results. But for your activities and experiments, the kitchen scale will be accurate enough.

Different scales
Kitchen scales are not accurate enough to show small differences in mass. A spring balance would show a difference of mass between these two spoonfuls of sugar.

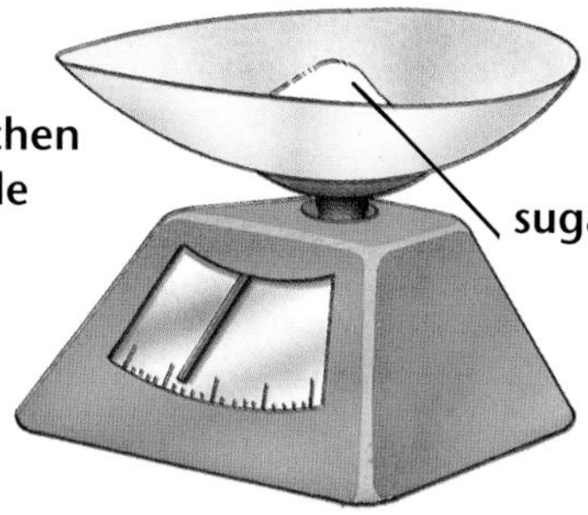

Measuring distance

You will not have all the different measuring equipment that a scientist might use to measure distance. But often it is possible to make your own. It will usually be accurate enough for the activities you will do.

Your ruler is probably one foot or one yard long. The yard has three feet and each foot has 12 inches. Some rulers are also marked for metric measurements in centimeters and millimeters. Is yours?

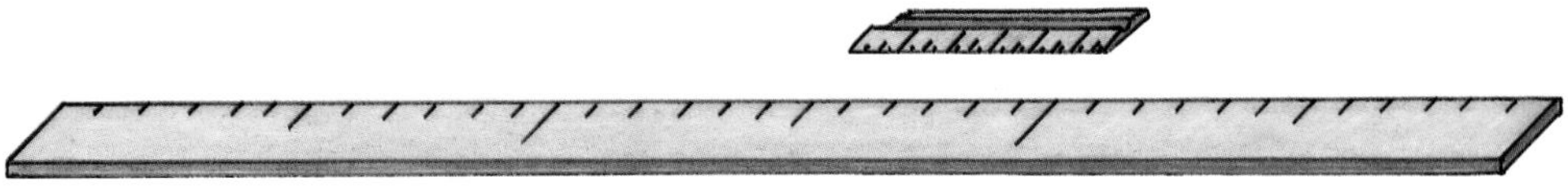

You can measure larger distances by using a rope with a knot tied at every yard.

If you need to measure something that is not a straight line, use a piece of string to measure it. Then mark or cut the string at the correct point and measure the length of string with a ruler.

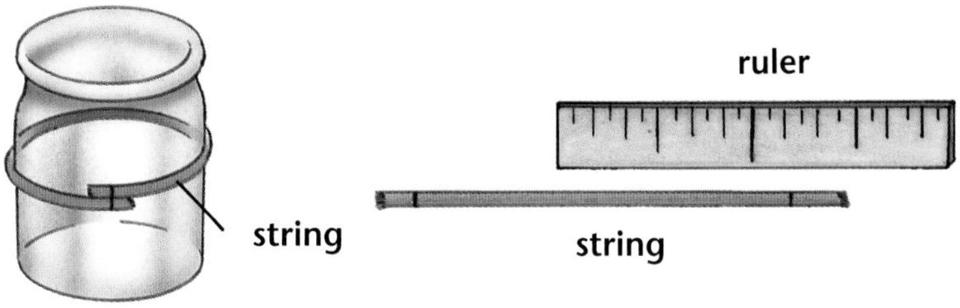

Guess the measurements

Here is a good way to practice using different units. Guess a measurement and then check to see how accurate your guess was. Guess how many inches wide this page is. Now measure it with your ruler. Feel how heavy you think this book is. Now check the answer by using some kitchen scales.

Make a chart like this. Two examples have been filled in for you. Don't forget to choose the units carefully. You will be surprised how quickly your guesses improve with practice.

Measuring	Guess	Actual
Width of the table.	32 inches	34 inches
Mass of a can of peaches.	12 ounces	14 ounces
Time taken for dripping tap to fill a bottle	?	?

Working safely

Making things and doing experiments can be a lot of fun. But it's easy to forget the most important thing—**safety.** Always remember that if you work carelessly, you could hurt yourself and other people.

Safety of yourself

If you're using sharp or heavy equipment, or using anything hot, remember to ask an adult for help.

Never play with electricity. Always use a battery with the correct voltage, which you will be told in the instructions. If you are not sure whether or not the battery you have is the correct one, check with an adult before you do the activity.

If you read through the instructions carefully before you start, you won't make mistakes and your experiments will be more successful.

Try to keep everything you use neat and in separate containers, with lids if necessary. If you are careful, you won't spill, break or drop things.

Never put anything in your mouth. Wash your hands after experiments involving chemicals and other substances.

Be extra careful not to get any powders or liquids in your eyes. If something does accidentally squirt or blow into your eyes, immediately tell an adult what has happened.

Think before you work

Think carefully before you start each step of an activity. By working slowly and carefully, your experiments will be safe and a lot more fun.

Safety of others

When you've finished your experiments, put everything away and make sure you leave the room clean.

Wipe the work surface and the floor in case you have spilled any sticky or slippery powders or liquids.

Safety symbol
When you see this triangle it means that the activity could be dangerous. You must follow the instructions inside the box very carefully.

Asking for help

Some activities in your *Young Scientist* books could be dangerous. You will need to use sharp or heavy tools, hot liquids, and other materials. All of these need special care and attention. So your *Young Scientist* books will often tell you to ask an adult to help you. You should always follow this piece of advice.

If, for example, you look on page 70 in **Planet Earth/Water,** you will see an activity in which you need to hammer a hole into the lid of a can. On page 104 of **Communication/Energy,** you will be told to cut into a cork. These are just two examples where an adult's help will make sure your activity is safe and fun. If there is something you don't understand, don't be afraid to ask. Adults can explain difficult ideas. They can show you how to use the glossary to find the meanings of new words, and how to use the index to find the volumes and the pages you need to look at. It will be interesting for them to see your work and join in the fun. Perhaps they can learn a thing or two from you!

Cumulative index

This index will help you find all the information on a topic in books **1** to **9**, and on pages 8 to 39 of book **10.** The topics are arranged in alphabetical order.

When you have found your topic entry, you will see numbers after the word—for example 3:30. The number listed first tells you which book to look in. The number that follows the colon tells you which page to look at. You may find the words "see also" followed by other topic entries. This is to help you find out more about a topic.

Page numbers in *italic* type are references to illustrations.

A

abacus, *7:68*
abdomen, of insect, 3:24–25
absorption
in plant, 1:88
of color, 4:18–19
abutment, 9:35
abyss, 6:26
AC, see **alternating current electricity**
acacia tree, *1:78*
acetic acid, 5:39
acetylene, 5:53, 5:104–105
acetylene torch, 5:104–105
acid, 5:24–25, 5:42, 6:30
acid rain, 2:98–99
action, of piano, 9:76
action and reaction, 6:114–115
Adélie penguin, *2:83*
adrenal gland, *2:45*
adrenalin, *2:45*
aerosol, 2:85
aerosol can, 5:32
Africa, 6:16, *6:85*
African elephant, *1:44, 1:60, 3:65, 3:107*

African elephant

African porcupine, *3:97*
African savanna, *1:78*
agar, *1:25*
agricultural scientist, *10:9*
agriculture, 1:111, *2:64, 2:116,* 6:92, *9:61*
careful methods, 2:92–93
intensive, 2:88–90
natural habitat and, 2:70–71, 2:90, 2:94–95
organic, 2:91
tallying in, 7:66–67
tropical rain forest and, 2:79
see also **fertilizer; pesticide**
AI, 7:117
aileron, 9:104–105
air, *5:8,* 5:26, 5:66–67, 6:14, 6:61
as insulator, 8:89

breathing of, see **breathing**
color and, 4:38–39
combustion and, 5:94–95
compressed, 5:52, 5:86–87, 5:102–103
distillation, 5:98–99
expansion of, 5:33
flying in, 5:76–77, 9:104
gases in, 5:68–69, 5:96–97
gas separation from, 5:52–53, 5:98–99
humidity, 5:107
in atmosphere, 5:70–71, 7:9
pollution in, see **air pollution**
pressure of, see **air pressure**
sound waves and, 8:78–79
uses for, 5:96–97
see also **gas; oxygen; wind**
airfoil, 5:76–77, 9:104
airplane, *5:95, 5:117, 8:65,* 9:104–105
computer in, 7:112
flight by, 5:76–77, 9:104–105
materials in, 6:54, 9:9
supersonic, 5:75
air pollution, 2:96–99, *2:117,* 6:61
air pressure, 5:80, 6:14, 6:38–39, 6:69
air separator, 9:101
airship, 5:75
Aland Islands, *6:117*
alarm, automobile, *7:89*
alarm clock, *7:87*
Alaska, *8:93*
albatross, *2:83*
alcohol, 8:115
Aldis lamp, 8:19
Aldrin, Edwin, 7:56
algae, 1:24, 3:46, 6:50
alginates, 6:50
alkali, 5:24–25, 5:42–43
alkaline battery, 4:54
allergy, 2:58
alley cropping, 2:93
alligator, 3:71
alloy, 4:80, 5:17, 5:44, 6:54
alnico, 4:80
aloe plant, *1:115*
alphabet, 8:14
Alpha Centauri, 7:14
alpha particle, 5:60
alpine tundra, 1:70
Alps, 6:19
alternating current electricity, *4:72,* 4:104–105
altitude, 5:70–71
air pressure and, 6:14–15
boiling of water and, 6:88
ALU, 7:92–93
aluminum, 5:50–51, 6:50, 6:54, 6:55, 9:12
aluminum oxide, 5:50, 6:111
aluminum wire, 4:80
alveoli, 2:17, 3:87
Amazonian water lily, *1:66*
Amazon River, 4:49
AM broadcasting, 8:37
ambulance, *8:53*
ameba, 1:9, 1:13, *1:15, 6:10*
as parasite, 1:55
food and, 1:23
movement, 1:23

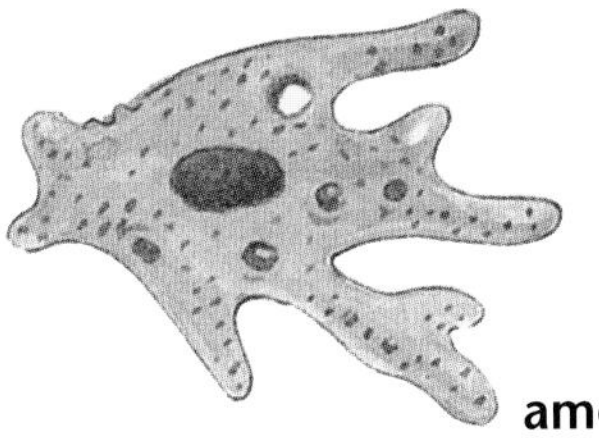
ameba

amebic dysentery, 1:55
amp, see **ampere**
ampere, 4:62–63
Ampère, André, 4:62
amphibian, *3:64,* 3:68–69, 3:80
amplifier, 8:40–41, 8:42, *8:47*
amplitude, 8:34
anchor arm, 9:37
Andes Mountains, 3:104
AND gate, 7:88–89
Andromeda Galaxy, 7:19
anemometer, 6:41
aneroid barometer, 5:80–81
angiosperm, 1:92
angle
of incidence, 4:27
of reflection, 4:29
of refraction, 4:27

angler fish, *3:64*
animal
blood movement in, 1:46
breathing by, 1:42, 5:68
cell of, 1:9, 1:18–21
classification, 1:12–13, 1:16
decomposition and, 1:32–35
defenses by, 1:56–57
development through time, 1:58–61
eating by, 1:36–39
electricity in, 4:49
endangered species, see **endangered species**
energy for, 8:90
extinct, 1:60, 2:72
farm, see **agriculture**
habitat destruction, 2:71
hormones in, 1:51
in food chain, 1:30–31
movement by, 1:48–50
nervous system in, 1:51
night vision of, 4:46–47
parasite, 1:54
polar regions, 2:82–83
protecting, 2:77
rain forest, 2:78, 2:81
reproduction by, 1:52–53
structure made by, 9:8
waste from, 1:40–41
see also **invertebrate; vertebrate;** specific animals
animation, 7:110–111
Annelida, 3:8, 3:15
annual, 1:108
answering machine, *7:87*, 8:9, 8:54

answering machine

ant, *3:43*
Antalya, Turkey, *6:68*
Antarctica, 2:82–84, *4:21*, 6:32–33, *6:90*
animals of, 3:103
Antarctic Circle, 6:42
Antarctic Treaty, 2:83
Antares, 7:14–15
anteater, 3:89
antelope, 1:31
antenna (device), 7:39, 7:40, *7:113*, 8:36–38, 8:42, *8:48*, 9:39
antenna, of insect, 3:25
anther, 1:94–95
anthracite, 8:96
antibody, 2:50
antilock brake system, 9:98
anus, 1:40, 2:24
anvil, ear, 2:28–29
aperture, camera lens, 4:35
aphid, 1:37, *1:56*, 3:42, 3:57
Apollo spacecraft, *7:34*, *7:45*, 7:56
appliance, household, 4:65, 8:66–67
applications software, 7:98–99
applied science, 10:11
aqualung, 5:103
aqueduct, *9:9*, *9:34*
arachnid, 3:22
arame, *1:25*
archaea, 1:13
archaeopteryx, 3:80, 3:82
arch bridge, 9:35
arch dam, 9:50–51
archer, *8:77*
Arches National Park, *6:31*
architect, 9:30
Arctic, 2:82, 3:102
Arctic Circle, 6:42
arctic fox, *2:82*, 3:102
arctic hare, *2:82*
arctic lichen, *1:29*
Arctic Ocean, *2:82*, 6:32, 6:33
arctic poppy, *2:82*
arctic skua, *2:82*
arctic tern, *3:94*

arctic tundra, 1:70
arc welding, *4:63*
area (measurement), 10:34
argon, 4:24, 5:68, 5:97, 5:99, 5:116, 6:14
arithmetic/logic unit, 7:92–93
arm, as lever, 9:72
armadillo, *3:97*
armature, 9:109
Armstrong, Neil, 7:56
array, 7:27
arrow-poison frog, *3:64, 3:97*
artery, 2:18, *2:20*
arthropod, 3:9, 3:22–29
Arthropoda, 3:9
artificial intelligence, 7:117
Asia, formation of, 6:18
Asian wart snake, *3:65*
asphalt, *9:52*
assembly line, 9:114
asteroid, 3:81, 7:20, 7:24, 7:58
astronaut, 5:96, 6:9, 7:44
  equipment for, 7:52–53, *7:113*
  moon landing by, 7:56–57
  space shuttle, 7:46
  space station, 7:54, 7:55
  training, 7:50–51
  weightlessness of, 7:49
  work of, 7:49, 7:52, *7:57*
  see also **space travel**
astronomer, 7:9, 10:21
athlete, *5:92*
Atlantic Ocean, 1:25
Atlantis (space shuttle), *7:32–33*, 7:47, 7:54
atmosphere, 5:70–71, 6:9, 6:14–15, *6:66*, 7:9
  not found on moon, 7:12
  sky color and, 4:38–39
  see also **air; weather**
atmospheric interference, see **signal**
atom, 5:10–11, 8:68
  conducted heat and, 8:88
  energy from, 8:73, 8:102
  excited, 4:25, 4:40
  hydrogen, 8:73
  in crystal, 5:22–23
  in element, 5:12–13
  in gas, 5:85
  in magnet, 4:88
  in molecule, 5:16–17
  light and, 4:24–25
  water, 6:84

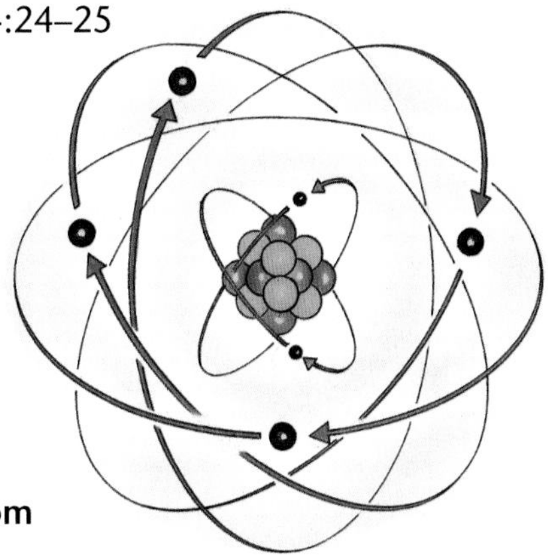

carbon atom

attraction and repulsion
  in electric charge, 4:56
  magnetic, 4:82–85, 4:110
aurora, 4:8
  australis, 4:87
  borealis, 4:87
Australia, *6:52*
automatic teller machine, 7:104
automatic transmission, 9:98
automobile, *2:114–115*
  alarm system, *7:89*
  assembly of, *9:114*
  brakes, 9:98
  energy for, *8:65*, 8:115
  engine, 9:67, 9:96
  generator in, *4:107*
  jack, 9:81
  mechanical system, 9:98–99
  radio, *8:39*
  road as inclined plane, 9:78
  rusting, *6:110*
autopilot, 7:112
autumn, 6:36–37
autumn crocus, 1:115
Aves, *3:65*
ax, 9:79
axis, of Earth, 6:36, 7:10
axle, 9:65, 9:82–87
axon, 2:40
Aztec architecture, 9:28, 9:29

B

baby, *2:66*
Babylonian architecture, 9:28, 9:35, 9:50
bacilli, *1:13*
backbone, see **spinal column**
backpack, for astronaut, 7:52–53
bacteria, 1:13, *1:15,* 1:26–27, 2:103, 5:110–111, *10:19*
decay and, 1:33
division, *1:52*
illness and, 2:48–49
infection and, 1:56
rod-shaped, *1:26, 1:27, 2:48*
spherical, *1:26*
spiral, *1:27*

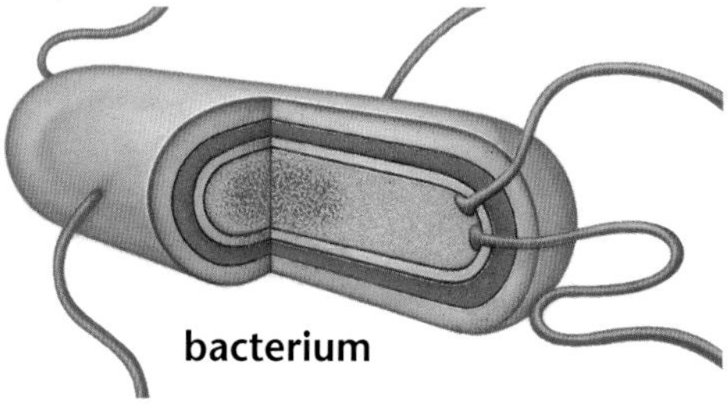

bacterium

Bactrian camel, *3:100*
baking soda, see **bicarbonate of soda**
balance (instrument), *5:34–35*
balance, sense of, 2:29, 2:38
bald cypress, 1:67
bald eagle, *3:105*
Bali, Indonesia, *6:77*
ball and socket joint, 2:14
ball-bearings, 9:71
balloon, 5:82, 5:85, 7:39
hot-air, *5:8,* 5:74, *6:15*
Baltimore oriole, *3:73*
bamboo, *1:110,* 2:72
banana, 8:74
bank card, *7:104*
Barbary ape, *10:14*
barb feather, 3:83
bar code, 7:104–105
bark, of tree, 1:72
bark beetle, 3:40–41
barley, 1:112
barnacle, 1:37
barn owl, *3:72*
barn swallow, 3:95
barometer, 5:80–81
basalt, 6:13
base, of transistor, 8:43
base 2, see **binary system**
base 10, 7:68
BASIC, 7:100, 7:101
bat (animal), *1:17, 3:78,* 3:92–93
battery, 4:52–55, 8:91, 8:93, 10:28
bauxite, 2:112, 5:50, 6:55, *6:61*
Bay of Fundy, 6:29
beam (construction), 9:23, 9:26
bear, *1:17, 3:89,* 3:102
polar, 2:75, *2:82, 3:96,* 3:102
Beaufort scale, 5:73
bee, *1:98, 2:58,* 3:27, *3:45,* 3:57, 4:47
beech tree, *1:12*
beetle, 1:35, *3:34,* 3:40–41, *3:44,* 3:58, *3:60*
Bell, Alexander Graham, 8:24
bench, *9:9*
benthos, 3:46
beryl, *5:22*
beta particle, 5:60
Betelgeuse, 7:14–15
bicarbonate of soda, 5:24, 5:25, 5:34–35, 5:38–39, 6:109
biceps, 1:48, 2:15
bicycle, *2:114–115, 2:117, 8:64,* 8:98, 9:86–87
brakes, 9:71, *9:87*
bicycle pump, 5:87
biennial, 1:108
"big-bang" theory, 5:108
Big Boy (steam engine), 9:93
Big Dipper, 4:90, 7:14
bilharzia, 3:15
binary system, 7:69, 7:81
biochemist, 10:21
biodegradable material, 2:111
biodiversity, 3:61
biogas, 8:116–117
biological clock, 2:27
biologist, 10:20
biology, 10:20
biomass, 8:114–117

Biosphere 9:2, *9:60*
bird, *1:12, 1:17,* 3:65, 3:72–73
feather insulation in, *9:58*
flight by, 3:82–83
ocean, 3:111
oil spills and, *2:102*
sleep of, 3:90
spreading seeds, *1:101*
waste from, 1:40
way of eating, 1:36

bird

Birmingham, England, *4:111*
birth, 2:47
bit, 7:88
bitter taste, 2:30
bitumen, 5:55, *5:112*
bivalve, 3:21, 3:53
black, *4:19*
black hole, 7:16, 7:29
black rhinoceros, *3:107*
bladder, 1:40, 2:19, 2:24–25
blast furnace, 5:45
blasting, 9:47
block and tackle, 9:89
blood, 1:46–47
blood, human, 2:9, 2:18–19
pumping by heart, 2:20–21
blood cell, *1:21*
blood poisoning, *1:26*
blood vessel, 1:46–47, 2:18
blubber, 3:98
blue (color), 4:16–17, 4:38–39, *4:115, 8:46–47, 8:49*
blue grama grass, *1:79*
Blue Lagoon, *8:113*
blue tit, *1:12*
blue whale, 2:75, *2:83, 3:74*
blue wildebeest, 3:95
boat, 6:103, 6:115, 6:117, *8:65*
bobbing cork, 6:98
bog, 1:81
boil, *1:26*
boiler, 8:100
boiling point, 5:30, 6:88
bolt, 9:80
bombardier beetle, 3:58
bone, 1:49
bone, human, 2:12–13
joints and, 2:14
muscles and, 2:15
bony fish, 3:64, 3:66
boom, 9:102
booster rocket, 7:34
bootlace worm, 3:14
bore (tool), 9:32
borer (tool), *9:113*
boring machine, 9:47
botanist, 10:20
bottle, *9:15*
bottled gas, 5:86–87, 5:112
bottling factory, *6:81*
bow and arrow, *8:77*
bowhead whale, *2:82*
box girder bridge, 9:35
brain, human, 2:9, *2:10*
coordination and, 2:38
hormones and, 2:44
messages to and from, 2:40–42
senses and, 2:26, 2:39
brain stem, 2:40
brain wave, 3:91
brakes
automobile, 9:98
bicycle, 9:71, *9:87*
branch flow chart, 7:78
Brazil, *2:80, 6:48*
Brazilian orchid, *1:75*
bread, 1:113, *6:79*
breast cancer, 2:59
breathing, 1:42–43, 2:16–17, 3:86, 5:88, 5:92–93

breathing (continued)
collecting breath underwater, 5:91
compressed air, 5:102–103
breathing apparatus, 5:102
brick, *8:87,* 9:20–21
bridge, *9:23,* 9:34–38
compression of, 9:16
material in, *9:9,* 9:26
brimstone butterfly, *3:32*
brittle star, *3:9*
broach, *9:112*
broadcasting
radio, 8:34–37
television, 8:47
bromine, 6:50
bronchiole, 3:87
bronchus, 2:16–17, 3:87
bronze, 6:54
brush (mechanical part), 4:106–107, 9:109
bryophyllum, 1:106
bryophyte, 1:64, 1:90
bud
plant, 1:106
sponge, 3:48
bug, computer, 7:100
building construction, see **structure**
bullhead fish, *1:53*
buoyancy, 6:106
bur, 1:101
Buran (space shuttle), 7:47
burglar alarm, 4:22
burrow, 9:8
burying beetle, *3:60*
bush cricket, *3:31*
butane, 5:86, 5:112
butterfly, *1:12,* 2:75, *3:9,* 3:28, *3:32,* 3:57, *5:8*
butterflyfish, *1:12, 3:110*
buttress, 9:25
buttress dam, 9:50–51
Buxton, United Kingdom, *6:81*
byte, 7:88

C

C (computer language), 7:100
cable, 4:59, *9:17,* 9:40
fiber optic, 8:57, 8:58
telecommunications, 8:32–33
telephone, 9:54
cable-stayed bridge, 9:36–37
cable television, 8:59
cactus, *1:57, 1:65,* 6:93, *10:9*
CAD, 7:110, 9:30
calcium, 2:12, 6:80
calcium carbonate, 6:108
calculation, 7:65, 7:70–71
by computer, 7:80–81, 7:112–113
with measurement, 7:73
"yes" and "no" answers in, 7:74–77
calculator, electronic, *4:116,* 7:82–83, *7:86, 8:44,* 8:107
California, 8:109
California condor, 2:75
caliper brakes, on bicycle, *9:87*
calorie, 8:74
cam, 9:97
cambered road, 9:55
camel, 1:60, *3:100*
camel spider, 3:44
camera, 4:34–35
television, 8:46–47, 8:58
camouflage, 1:57, 3:96, 3:102

green chameleon

camphor, 1:115
camshaft, 9:97
cancellous bone, 2:12–13
cancer, 2:59
candle, *4:10*

canine, 3:88–89
canopy, 1:74
cantilever arm, 9:37
cantilever bridge, 9:37
canyon, 6:30
Capella, *7:14*
Cape Mountains, 6:16
capillary, 2:17, *2:23,* 3:86–87
capillary action, 6:97
Capitol, U.S. (building), 9:48–49
car, see **automobile**
carbohydrate, 1:38, 2:22, 8:74
carbon, 1:45, 5:37, 5:55, *5:57,* 6:54
  atom of, *5:12, 5:58*
  in telephone, 8:25
carbonated drink, 5:88–89, 5:97
carbon dioxide, 3:86, 5:39, 5:41
  as waste, 1:40–41, 2:24
  breathing and, 1:43, 1:45
  carbonation and, 5:88–89
  density of, 5:78–79
  distillation, 5:99
  erosion by, 6:30
  forest destruction and, 2:79
  greenhouse effect and, 2:86–87
  in air, 5:68, 6:14
  in blood, 2:20
  in breathing, 2:16–17
  in smelting, 5:45
  plants and, 1:12, 1:82, 1:84
  uses of, 5:97
  yeast and, 1:113

carbon dioxide

carbonic acid, 5:24
carbon monoxide, 2:97, 5:45
carcinogen, 2:59
cardiac muscle, 2:15
caribou, *2:82*
carnivore, 1:30–31, 1:36, 3:89
carpenter's brace, *9:83*
carrier wave, 8:36–37
carrot, *1:110*
cartilage, 2:13, 3:66
cartilaginous fish, 3:66
cartoon, 7:110
cassette player, 8:9
cassette tape, *4:79*
Cassini (space probe), 7:58
cassiterite, 6:55
casting mold, *5:51*
cat, *1:50,* 2:71, *3:65, 3:87,* 3:92, *8:79*
  lung of, *3:87*
  wild, *1:17*
catalyst, 5:57
catalytic converter, 2:97
catapult, 9:74–75
caterpillar (insect), 3:28–29
caterpillar (machine), 9:116–117
cattle, 2:89
cave, 6:30
CD-ROM, 7:84, 7:85, *7:93,* 7:97, *7:99,* 7:111
cell (area), 8:52
cell (living thing)
  animal, 1:9, 1:18–21
  as unit of life, 1:9
  bacteria, *1:27*
  blood, 2:18, *2:51*
  division, 1:20–21
  food for, 1:21, *1:46*
  making model of, 1:18
  muscle, 2:11
  nerve, 2:10–11, 2:40
  parts of, 1:18–19, 2:10
  plant, 1:9, 1:21, 1:84
  reproductive, 1:94
  shape, 1:20
  size, 1:20
  splitting, 1:52

cell, battery, 4:54
cellophane, 5:94
cellular telephone, 8:52
cell wall, 1:19, *1:27*
cement, 9:22–23
centimeter, 10:33–34
centipede, *3:9,* 3:22
central processing unit, 7:92–93, *7:97*
centrifuge, *7:51*
Cephalaspidomorphi, *3:64*
Ceres, 7:23
CFC's, 2:85
chaffinch, *3:65*
chain reaction, 8:102–103

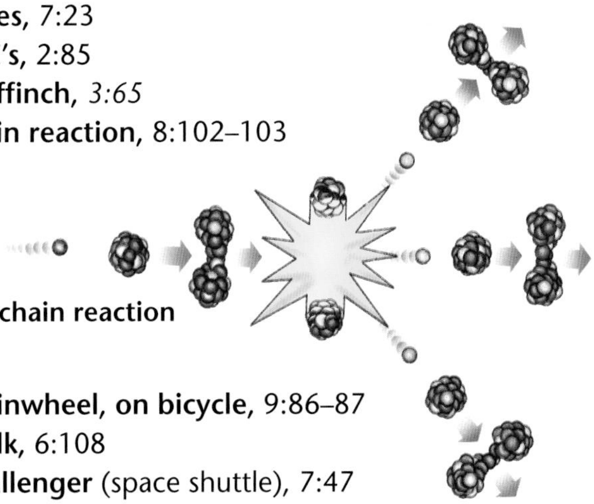
chain reaction

chainwheel, on bicycle, 9:86–87
chalk, 6:108
Challenger (space shuttle), 7:47
chamber (Earth), 6:22
chameleon, *3:96*
Channel Tunnel, 9:46–47
chanterelle, *1:28*
chaparral, 1:76–77
Chappe, Claude, 8:14
charge-coupled device, *8:46*
Charon, 7:23
cheetah, 3:107
chelonian, 3:71
chemical change, 5:37–39, 8:71
chemical element, see **element**
chemical energy, 8:70–71, 8:84, 8:90
chemical fertilizer, 2:90, 2:91
chemical pesticide, see **pesticide**
chemical reaction, 5:20, 5:40–43, 5:48
chemical weedkiller, 2:90
chemist, *10:9,* 10:20, 10:21
chemistry, *10:9,* 10:20
Chernobyl explosion, 2:104–105
chess, 7:116
chest cavity, *2:20*
Chicago, 9:42
chicken liver sponge, *3:8*
chimera, *3:64*
chimney, *9:92*
China, *8:116*
  Great Wall of, *9:29*
chip, electronic, 7:86–87, *7:97,* 8:42, 8:44–45
chlamydomonas, 1:24
chlorine, *5:13, 5:16–17,* 5:19, 5:20, 5:47, 6:75
chlorococcum, 1:24
chlorofluorocarbons, 2:85
chlorophyll, 1:21, 1:84
chloroplast, 1:21, 1:84
cholera, 2:52
Chondrichthyes, *3:64*
Chordata, 3:64
chromium, 5:49, *6:61*
chrysalis, 3:28
cilia, 1:22
ciliate, 1:22
circuit, see **electric circuit; electronic circuit; integrated circuit**
circuit breaker, 4:69
cirque, 6:34–35
citrus swallowtail butterfly, *3:28*
city, 2:67, *9:11*
  of the future, 9:60
  sealed, 9:60–61
  skyscrapers, 9:42–43
  underground, 9:54–55
  water use in, 6:76
civil engineer, 10:21
cladding, 9:42
clam, 3:21
class (biology), 1:16, 3:64–65
classification, of life, 1:12–17
clay, 9:20
cleanliness, *2:56,* 2:61
clean room, 8:45
climate, 6:42–43
climatologist, 6:42
climbing plant, 1:75
clinker, 9:22
clock, *7:72, 7:87,* 9:69, 9:84–85, *10:36*
  in computer, 7:93

spring in, 8:91
clockwise movement, *9:83*
clockwork, 9:84
clothing, protective, 9:14
cloud, *6:38*, 6:65
formation of, 6:44
lightning and, 6:44
tornado and, 6:46
club fungus, *1:13*
club moss, *1:12*, *1:64*
cluster (star), 7:15
Cnidaria, 3:8, 3:12–13
coal, 4:74, 6:60–61
energy from, 8:64, 8:67, 8:92, 8:96–97, 8:101
coal gas, 5:113
coast
climate on, 6:43
shape of, 6:29
cobalt, 4:80, 6:51
COBOL, 7:100
cobra, *3:116*
cocci, *1:13*, *1:15*
cochlea, *2:26*, 2:28
cockle, *3:9*
cockpit, 9:104
cocoa, *1:110*
coconut, *1:110*
cocoon, 3:37
coding and decoding
Morse, 8:17, 8:21
telephone, 8:29
coffee, *1:111*
cog, 9:83, 9:84
coke, 5:45, 5:113
coke oven gas, 5:113
colchicine, 1:115
cold, see **temperature; temperature changes**
cold, sensing, 2:32
cold-blooded animal, 3:98
collecting gas over water, 5:90–91
collector, on transistor, 8:43
colony
algae, 1:24
coral, 3:13
termite, 3:26
color, 4:11, 4:14–19
absorption and, 4:18–19
broadcasting in, 8:46–47
of sky, 4:38–39
primary, 4:16–17
printing in, 9:111
reflection and, 4:18–19
seeing, 2:35
see also **light; spectrum**
Colorado River, 6:30
Columbia (space shuttle), 7:47
combustion, 5:94–95, 7:32
see also **fire**

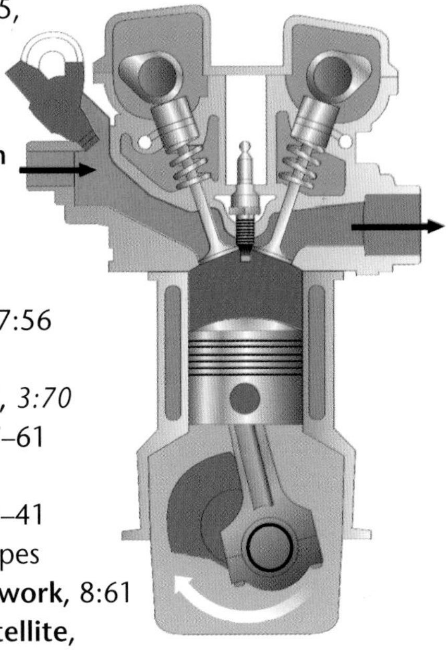

combustion engine

comet, 7:20, 7:25
command module, 7:56
common tern, *3:73*
common wall lizard, *3:70*
communication, 8:7–61
definition of, 8:9
with satellite, 7:40–41
see also specific types
communication network, 8:61
communications satellite, 7:38, 8:23, 8:26, 8:27, 8:50–51
danger to, 8:51
geostationary, 8:50
radio broadcast from, 8:27, 8:35
relay, 8:13
television broadcast from, 8:48, 8:59
commutator, *4:104*, 9:109
Comoro Islands, *3:115*
compact bone, 2:12–13
compacting machine, 9:52
compass, magnetic, *4:79*, 4:87, 4:90–91
compost, 2:110, 2:114–115
compound, 5:20–21, 6:52
compound eye, 4:47
compression, 5:52, 5:86–87, 5:102–103, 9:16–17, 9:22–23
compressor, 9:95

computer, 7:63–117, *10:17*
controlling, 7:94–95
database, 7:106–107
in aircraft, 7:112
in design, 9:30
in network, 7:107–109
in printing, 9:111
in spacecraft, 7:39–40, 7:113
memory, 7:96–97
speed of, 7:80
systems, 7:84–85, 7:92–93
thinking by, 7:80–81, 7:88–89, 7:116–117
types of, 7:90–91
uses for, 7:65, 7:104–105
writing by, 7:102–103
see also **Internet**
computer-aided design, 7:110, 9:30
computer game, *7:98*
computer graphics, 7:110
computer program, 7:81, 7:84, 7:98–102
computer software, 7:84, 7:98–102
concave lens, 4:32–33
conch, *3:60*
concrete, 9:19, 9:22–23
in oil platform, *9:40*
in skyscrapers, 9:42
on steel frame, 9:26
reinforced, 9:23, 9:47
condensation, *5:30–31*, 5:32, 5:98, 5:106, 6:86–88, 8:69
in cloud formation, 6:44
in water cycle, 6:66
condenser, 8:100
condor, 2:75
conduction, see **conductor**
conductor
of electricity, 4:50–51, 4:59, 4:112, 5:15, 5:46, 8:42
of heat, 6:89, 8:88–89
cone, *1:93*, 1:96–97, 9:10–11
cones, in eye, 2:35
conifer, 1:73, 1:93
conservation, 1:116–117, 2:63–117, 2:68
constellation, 7:14–15
container, 9:14–15
continent, 6:13
movements, 6:16
continental drift, 6:16
continental Morse code, 8:17
continental shelf, 6:26
contour plowing, 2:93
contraction, 5:29, 5:84–85
muscle, 2:15
control center, 7:40
control unit, 7:92–93
convection, 6:89
convection current, 6:44, 6:89
convergence, 4:32
converter, of energy, 8:84, 8:98
convex lens, 4:32–33
conveyor belt, 9:114
cooking, *8:67*, 8:84
cooling equipment, 6:76
cooling tower, 8:100
coordination, body, 2:38
copper, 5:48–49, 6:51, 6:52, 6:54, 6:55, *6:61*, *9:26*
copper mine, *2:101*
copper wire, 4:59, 4:111
coral, 1:12, *3:8*, 3:13, 3:46–47, 3:54–55
coral reef, 3:13, 3:54–55
cordless telephone, 8:53
core
of Earth, 6:12–13, 6:17
of skyscraper, 9:42
of sun, 8:95
soil, 9:32
corn, *1:110*, *2:88*
cornea, *2:34*
corn poppy, *1:92*
corrosion, 6:110–111
corundum, 6:56
cosmonaut, 7:44
cotoneaster, *1:101*
cotton, 5:94
coughing, *2:49*, *2:57*
counterclockwise movement, *9:83*
counterweight, 9:106
counting, 7:66–69
cow, 1:39

cowslip, *1:52*
CPU, see **central processing unit**
crab, *3:9*, 3:22–23, 3:46–47, 3:50, 3:53
crab spider, *3:22*
crane (machine), 4:95, *9:9*, 9:39, *9:88*
cranium, 3:64
crank, on bicycle, 9:86–87
crankshaft, 9:96, *9:97*
crater, 7:13, 7:24–25
crayfish, *1:46*
crewed spacecraft, 7:44
cricket, *3:31*, *3:44*
crocodile, *1:51*
crocodilian, 3:71
crocus, *1:109*, 1:115
crop, *6:92*
  see also **agriculture**
crop rotation, 2:93
crossbeam, 9:74
crown-of-thorns starfish, 3:55
crude oil, 5:54
crust (Earth), 6:12–13, 6:17, 6:19
  minerals in, 6:52–53
crustacean, 3:22, 3:32, 3:37, 3:50
crustose lichen, 1:29
crystal, 5:22–23, 5:34, 6:24, 6:56, 9:22
CU, 7:92–93
cube, 9:10–11, 10:35
cubic foot, 10:35
cud, 1:39
cullet, 2:112
cup fungus, *1:13*
current, electric, see **electric current**
cut, on skin, *2:57*
cut-and-cover tunneling, 9:47
cutting (plant), 1:52
cutting, of metals, 5:104–105
cuttlefish, 3:20
cycad, 1:93
cyclone, 6:47
cylinder, 9:10–11, 9:44
  hydraulic, 9:103
  piston, 9:96
  printing, 9:111
cytoplasm, 1:18–19, *1:27*, *1:46*, 2:10

D

dam, 6:116, 8:104, 9:50–51
damper, on piano, *9:76*
damp proofing, 9:56–57
damsel fly, *3:23*
dandelion seed, *1:100*
dandelion stem, *9:8*
darkling beetle, *3:44*
data, 7:85, 7:105, 10:12
database, 7:106–107
data glove, 7:111
data sheet, 6:59
day, 6:36
DC, see **direct current electricity**
decay and decomposition, 1:32–35, 3:16, 5:110–111
decibel, 8:79
deciduous tree, 1:72, 1:73
decimal system, 7:68
deck, 9:40
decomposition,
  see **decay and decomposition**
deep-sea diver, *5:102*
defenses, plant and animal, 1:56–57, 3:96–97
delta, 6:31
dendrite, 2:40
density, 5:78–79, 6:102–103, 6:106–107, 10:35
dermis, 2:33
desalination, 6:49
desert, 1:71, 2:94–95, 6:93, 9:60–61
  invertebrates in, 3:44–45
  vertebrates in, 3:100–101
desert cricket, *3:44*
desert locust, *3:9*
desert mirage, *4:27*
desert plant, 1:71
desert scorpion, 3:44
desert snake, *3:101*
desert toad, *3:101*
design, of building, 9:30–31
detergent, 2:103
deuterium, 8:73
Devonshire cup coral, *3:8*

diamond, 6:56–57
diaphragm, *2:16–17*
camera, 4:35
loudspeaker, 4:101
radio speaker, 8:41
telephone, 8:25

diary, naturalist's, 3:30–31
diesel fuel, 5:55, *5:112*
digestion, 1:38–39, 2:22–23, 8:74
digestive juices, 2:22–23
digit, 7:68, 7:88
digital computer, 7:65
see also **computer**
digitalis, 1:114
digital watch, *7:86, 10:36*
dilution, 6:48
dinosaur, 1:60, 3:80–81, 6:11
diplocaulus, 3:80
direct current electricity, 4:52, 4:104–105
direct reduction, 5:44
disc brakes, 9:98
Discovery (space shuttle), *5:83*, 7:47, *7:52*
disease, 2:48–61
causes, 2:48–49, 2:54–55
crop, 2:88, 2:90
from birth, 2:58
immune system and, 2:50–53
prevention, 2:52, 2:56–57, 2:61
dish antenna, 7:28, *7:113*
disk drive, 7:84, 7:97
dissolved substance, 6:80, 6:104
distance, 10:32, 10:37
and machines, 9:67
distillation, 5:98–99, 6:49
see also **fractional distillation**
distillation column, 5:112–113
divergence, 4:32
diving beetle, *3:34*
division, 7:71
docking port, 7:54
dodder stem, *1:55*
dog, *1:17, 3:79,* 3:92
dolomite, 6:108
dolphin, 3:90, 3:110, *3:117*
domain, magnet, 4:88, 4:98
dome, 9:48–49
doorbell, 4:96–97
dormancy, of tree, 1:73
dormouse, *3:91*, 8:90
dot matrix printer, 7:103
dots and dashes, see **Morse code**
down feather, 3:83
downloading, 7:109, 8:60
dragonfly, 3:34
drone bee, 3:27
drought, 2:95
drum brakes, 9:98
dryad's saddle, *1:28*
dry ice, 5:84, 5:97
drying clothes, 6:87
duck, 3:113
duck-billed platypus, *3:75*
dulse, *1:25*
dung beetle, 1:35
dunlin, *3:90*
Dutch elm disease, *3:40*
DVD, 7:84, 7:85, 7:97
dwarf goby, *3:66*
dwarf willow, *1:70*
dynamo, 8:98
see also **generator**

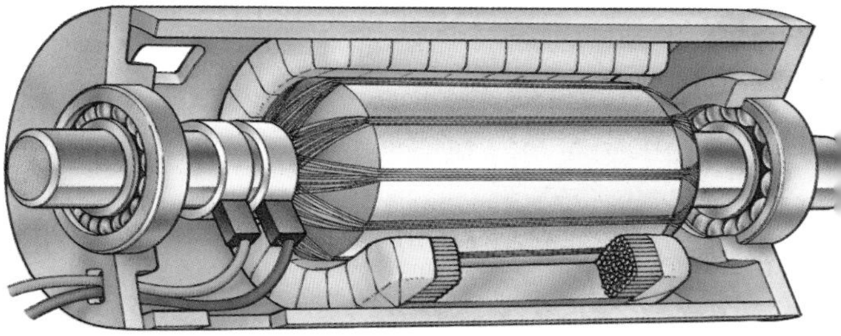

E

eagle, 2:75, *3:72*, 3:105
ear
  human, *2:26*, 2:28–29
  snake, *1:14*
ear canal, 2:28
eardrum, 2:28
ear flap, 2:28
earpiece, on telephone, 8:25
ear protective gear, *8:79*
Earth, 6:8–61
  age, 6:10
  appearance from space, *6:9*
  atmosphere of, see **atmosphere**
  climate of, 6:42–43
  compared to sun, 7:11
  gravitation of, 7:30
  human population on, 2:65–66
  ice on, 6:32–35
  inside of, 6:12–13, 8:112
  in solar system, 7:20–23
  life on, 1:11, 6:10
  magnetic field of, 4:86–87
  motions of, 6:36–37, 7:10
  origins of, 6:10–11
  size of, 6:9
  surface of, 6:9
  temperature on, 7:11, 7:42
  see also **conservation**
earthquake, 6:20–21
Earth-survey satellite, 7:38, 7:42
earthworm, 1:37, *1:47, 3:8,* 3:15–17, 3:37
ear trumpet, 8:11
eating, 3:88–89
  as sign of life, 1:11
  ways of, 1:36–37
  see also **digestion; food**
echinoderm, 3:9, 3:18–19
Echinodermata, 3:9
echolocation, 3:92–93
echo sounder, 6:27
eel, *3:64, 3:85, 3:94,* 4:49
egg, 1:53, 1:94
  chicken, 6:106, 8:74
  human, 2:46
  jellyfish, 3:49
egg-eating snake, *3:70*
egg sac, 3:36
Egyptian architecture, 9:28, 9:50
Egyptian vulture, *3:65*
Eiffel Tower, *9:38*
electrical charge, 4:54, 4:56
electric buzzer, 4:96–97, 4:114
electric circuit, 4:52–53, 8:20
  battery, 4:54–55
  safety of, 4:68–69
  short, 4:67
electric current, 4:50–51, 4:104–105
  charge of, 4:54, 4:56
  in circuit, 4:52–55
  in heating appliance, 4:65
  in telegraph, 8:17
  in telephone, 8:25–29
  in wire, 4:58–59
  measuring, 4:60–63
  metal and, 5:14, 5:15
  substance from, 5:46–51
  switching on and off, 4:66
  transformer and, 4:72–73
electric eel, 4:49
electricity, 4:49–75
  alternative sources, 4:74–75
  energy from, 8:64, 8:67, 8:92, 8:98
  for telecommunications, 8:9
  from dam, 9:50
  generating, 4:70–71, 8:98
  in living thing, 2:40, 4:49
  lightning and, 6:44
  uses for, 4:49
  see also **electric circuit; electric current; energy; power station**
electric motor, 4:104–105, 4:111, 9:108–109
electric telegraph, see **telegraph**
electric traction elevator, 9:106
electric train, *4:105*
electrode, 4:54, 5:48–49
electrodynamic maglev train, 4:110
electrolysis, 5:50–51

electrolyte, 4:54

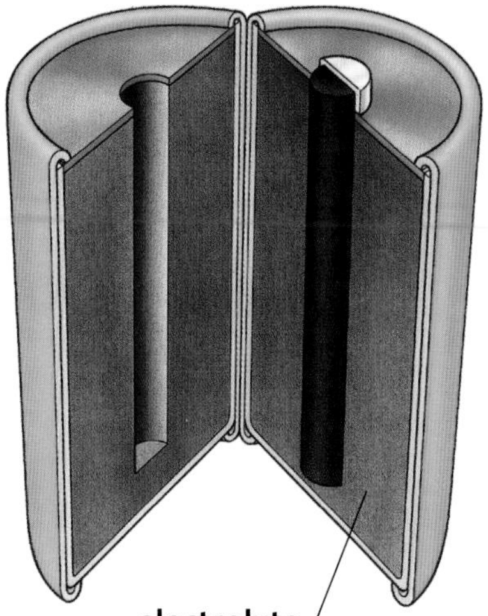

electromagnet, 4:92–117, 9:109
  in electric buzzer, 4:96–97, 4:114
  in electric motor, 4:104–105
  in generator, 4:106–107
  in metal detector, 4:102–103
  in radio, 8:41
  in scrapyard, 4:94
  in telegraph, 8:16, 8:20
  in telephone, 8:25
  levitation by, 4:108–111
  making, 4:92–93
  moving metals with, 4:95
  solenoid as, 4:98–101
  superconductivity and, 4:112–113
electromagnetic energy, 8:80–81
electromagnetic maglev train, 4:110
electromagnetic radiation, 4:114–117
electromagnetic spectrum, 4:20, 4:116–117
electromagnetic wave, 4:20, 4:115, 8:80–81
electron, 5:10–13, 8:73
  electrical charge and, 4:56
  light and, 4:24–25
electron gun, 8:48–49
electronic circuit, *8:42,* 8:44, 8:48
electronic mail, see **e-mail**
electron microscope, 5:10, 10:18–19
electroplating, 5:48–49
element, 5:12–15, 5:20, 6:52
elephant, *1:44, 1:60, 3:65, 3:74, 3:99, 3:107, 6:78*
elephantiasis, *2:55*
elephant seal, *2:83*
elevation (plan), 9:31
elevator
  airplane, 9:104–105
  building, 9:106–107
  grain, *9:45*
elevator shaft, 9:106–107
elliptical galaxy, 7:19
e-mail, 7:65, 7:107, 8:60
embankment dam, 9:50–51
embryo, plant, 1:94
emission, of light, 4:10–11, 4:25, 4:40
emitter, on transistor, 8:43
emperor penguin, *2:83,* 3:103
enclosure, 9:8
encoder, *8:47*
encyclopedia, electronic, *7:106*
endangered species, 2:72–75
  invertebrate, 3:60–61
  plants, 1:116–117
  vertebrate, 3:116–117

Komodo dragon

Endeavour (space shuttle), *7:29, 7:45,* 7:46, 7:47
endoscope, 4:44
energy, 5:9, 8:63–117, 9:90–92
  changing forms, 8:82–85
  chemical, 8:70–71, 8:84, 8:90
  definition of, 8:64–65
  electromagnetic, 8:80–81
  food and, see **food**
  fossil fuel, 6:60–61, 8:67, 8:96–97
  from water, see **water**
  geothermal, 8:112–113
  in home, 8:67
  kinetic, 8:68–69, 8:84, 8:86, 8:91, 8:98, 8:104,
    9:90
  machine and, 9:65, 9:67
  mechanical, 9:90

nuclear, see **nuclear energy**
potential, 8:76–77, 8:84, 9:90
radiant, 4:20
solar, see **solar energy; sun**
sound, 8:78–79
sources, 2:99, 4:74–75
storing, 1:31, 8:77, 8:90–91, 8:93
supplying, 8:92–93
wind, *8:64,* 8:67, 8:92, 8:108–109
work and, 8:86–87
see also **electricity**
energy converter, 8:84, 8:98
engine
automobile, *9:99*
internal combustion, 9:96–97
piston, 9:96–97
steam, 9:90–93
engineer, civil, 10:22
envelope, of airship, 5:75
enzyme, 1:19, *1:39, 2:22,* 2:33, 8:74
epidermis, 2:33
epiglottis, *2:23*
epiphyte, 1:75
Epsom salt, 6:56
equator, 4:90, 6:42, 7:73
equipment, for science, 10:24–25, 10:28–29, 10:36–37
equitorial orbit, *7:36*
ermine, *1:17*
Eros (asteroid), 7:58
erosion, 6:30–31
ERTS (satellite), 7:42
ESA, see **European Space Agency**
escapement, 9:84, 9:85
escape velocity, 7:36
escape wheel, on pendulum clock, *9:84*
esophagus, *2:16*
ethanol, 8:115
ethylene, 5:57
Etruscan shrew, *1:44*
eucalyptus, *1:99, 2:72*
euglena, 1:22
Eurasian kingfisher, *3:65*
Europa, 7:58
European lynx, 2:75
European Space Agency, 7:29, 7:54, 7:58
EVA, 7:52
evaporation, 5:21, 5:32, 5:84, 6:48–49, 6:86–87
in water cycle, 6:66
sweating as, 2:33, 3:99
evening star, 7:22
evergreen, 1:72, 1:74
exercise, physical, 2:61
exhaling, 1:42, 2:16–17, 5:92
exhaust gas, *9:97*
exoskeleton, 1:49, 3:22, 3:50
exosphere, 5:71, 6:14–15
expansion, of matter, 5:29, 5:32–33, 5:84–85
experiment, 10:13
expert system, 7:117
explosion, 5:32
expressway, 9:52
external combustion engine, 9:93
extinction, 1:60, 2:72, 3:81, 3:116
see also **endangered species**

dinosaur

extravehicular activity, 7:52
eye
animal, 2:36, 4:46–47
human, *2:26,* 2:34–37
eye, of hurricane, 6:47
eyepiece, telescope, 4:30

F

facsimile machine, 7:41, 8:9, 8:23
fact, 10:13
factory, 6:76, *6:81,* 7:114, *9:95*
fairy bonnet, *1:28*
fairy ring, 1:29
fall, see **autumn**
family, 1:16
fanworm, *1:36*

Faraday, Michael, 4:106
Far Infrared and Submillimeter Telescope, 7:29
farming, see **agriculture**
fat, 1:39, 2:22, 8:74
fat-tailed swamp wallaby, *3:75*
fatty layer, of skin, 2:33
fault, 6:19
fault-block mountain, 6:19
fax machine, see **facsimile machine**
feather, on bird, 3:83–84, *9:58*
feces, 1:40, 2:24
feldspar, *5:22*
fern, *1:12,* 1:64, 1:91, 1:107, *8:97*
fertilization, 1:53, 1:97
fertilizer, 2:88, 2:90, 2:91, 5:53, 6:92
fetus, 2:46–47
fiber, in diet, 2:22
fiberglass, 8:89, 9:19, 9:58
fiber optics, *4:9,* 4:44–45, 8:57, 8:58
field, in database, 7:106
field of vision, 4:46
filament, 4:64
film, photographic, 4:23, 4:34
filter feeder, 1:37
filtration tank, *6:83*
fin, 3:66
Finland, *6:117*
fire, 5:94–95, 6:114–115, 8:84, 9:102
  chaparral, 1:76
  grassland, 1:78
  in building, 9:26
  see also **combustion**
fireboat, 6:115
fire extinguisher, 5:95, 5:97
firefighting, *5:95,* 5:103, 6:114–115, 8:89, 9:102
fire hose, 6:114–115
firethorn, *1:65*
fireworks, *5:40,* 7:32, 8:70–71
Firth of Forth railway bridge, *9:37*
fish, *1:12, 1:17,* 3:66–67, 3:80, 3:92, 3:112
  as food, 6:50
  blood of, *1:47*
  breathing by, 5:88
  fossil, *1:58*
  ocean, 3:110
  origins of, 6:11
  pollution and, 2:102, 2:103
  reproduction, *1:53*
  streamlined, 6:101
  swimming of, 3:84–85
fisherman, *6:50*
fission, nuclear, 8:73, 8:102
fissure, 6:23
fixed joint, 2:14
flag, signaling with, 8:14
flagellate, *1:13*
flagellum, 1:22, *1:27,* 3:49
flap, airplane, 5:76
flare, solar, 7:11
flashlight, 4:52
flat-plate collector, 8:106
flatworm, *3:8,* 3:15
flea, *1:54, 3:9*
flight
  by airplane, 5:76–77
  by bird, 3:82–83
flight feather, 3:83
floating, 6:102–103, 6:107
  see also **hot-air balloon**
flooding, *6:43*
floor plan, 9:31
floppy disk, *7:85, 7:97, 7:99*
flour, 1:112
flow chart, 7:78
flower, 1:92
  desert, *1:71*
  parts of, *1:94*
  perfect versus imperfect, *1:94*
  scent, 1:98

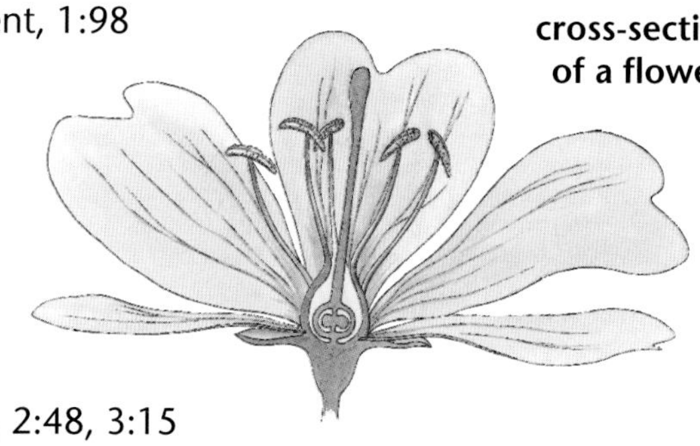

cross-section of a flower

fluke, 2:48, 3:15
fluorescent light, 4:10–11, 4:24
fluorine, 6:80
flux line, 4:85

fly, *2:56,* 3:57
tsetse, 2:54
fly agaric, *1:13, 1:28*
flying squirrel, 3:108
flywheel, 8:91
FM broadcasting, 8:37
foam carton, 2:85
focus
camera, 4:35
telescope, 4:31
fog, *6:85*
fold mountain, 6:19
foliose lichen, 1:29
food
ameba and, 1:23
as nutrient, 2:19
bacteria and, 1:27
balanced diet, 2:60
blood and, 1:46
energy from, *8:64,* 8:71, 8:74, 8:75, 8:90
for animals, 1:33, 1:39, 1:44–45
for humans, 1:21, 2:9, 2:22
for plant, 6:92
from ocean, 6:50
fruit as, 1:110
fuel for cooking, 8:67
grass as, 1:112–113
insect as, *1:11*
mushroom as, 1:28
root as, 1:110
safety, *2:57*
see also **digestion; eating; photosynthesis**
food chain, 1:30–31, 2:71, 2:103
foot (measurement), 10:32
foot, webbed, 3:113
football, *9:14, 9:68*
foot pedal, on piano, 9:76–77
forager bee, 3:27
force, 6:114–115, 8:86
machine and, 9:67–69
block and tackle, 9:89
inclined plane, 9:78
lever, 9:72–73
pulley, 9:88
screw, 9:80–81
wedge, 9:79
on structures, 9:16–17, 9:22–23, 9:42
see also **compression; friction; tension**
forest, 1:72–73, *1:116, 2:117*
see also **tropical rain forest; woodland**
fork, on bicycle, *9:87*
Fortran, 7:100
fossil, 1:58–60, 6:16, 6:18, 10:14
fossil, fern, *8:97*
fossil fuel, 6:60–61, 8:67, 8:96–97
fossil record, 1:59
foundation, 9:32–33
skyscraper, 9:42
four-cylinder engine, 9:97
four-stroke cycle, 9:97
fox, *1:30, 2:82, 3:89,* 3:102
foxglove plant, *1:114*
fractional distillation, 5:52, 5:54–55, 5:112–113
fractionating column, 5:52–53, *5:55*
framework, 9:26, 9:42
France, *6:108*
and Channel Tunnel, 9:46
Freedom 7 (spacecraft), 7:44
freeway, 9:52
freeze-thaw, 6:34–35
freezing, 5:28–29
freezing point, 5:28, 6:90
frequency, 4:115, 8:34
fresh water, 6:49, 6:106
fish, 3:67, 3:112
habitat, 3:34–35, 3:112
shrimp, *3:34*
friction, 7:23, 7:37, 9:67, 9:70–71
heat from, 9:71, 9:113
in brake, 9:87
frog, *1:17, 3:64,* 3:68–69, *3:79,* 3:109
frond, *1:64,* 1:91
front, weather, 6:46
frost, *5:106*
fruit, 1:101, 1:110
fruticose lichen, 1:29
fuel, 5:82–83, 5:112–115, 8:65, 8:101, 9:67
aircraft, *8:65*
biomass, 8:114–117
fossil, 6:60–61, 8:67, 8:96–97

fuel (continued)
rocket, 7:32–33
see also **energy; gasoline; natural gas; oil; petroleum**
fuel tank, 7:46
fulcrum, 9:72
Fuller, Buckminster, 9:49
full moon, 7:13
function (mathematics), 7:82
fungi, 1:28–29
classification of, 1:13
decay and, 1:34
parasite, 1:55
funnel cloud, 6:46
fuse, electric, 4:68–69

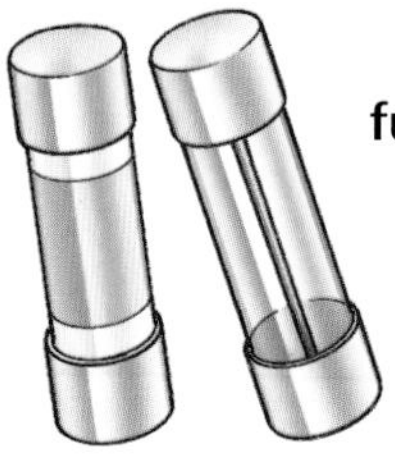

fuses

fusing, of metals, 5:104–105
fusion, nuclear, 5:109, 8:73, 8:95, 8:102

G

Gagarin, Yuri, 7:44
Galapagos Islands, 3:114
galaxy, 7:18–19
Galileo (space probe), 7:58
Galileo Galilei, 7:26, 7:100
gall, 3:41
gallery (insect tunnel), 3:41
gamma ray, 5:60, *8:80*
gamma-ray telescope, 7:29
gamma wave, 4:116
garbage, see **waste**
garden, 1:100, 2:70
garden spider, *3:9*
Garisar Gate, *6:74*
garnet, *5:22*
gas, 5:52, 5:63–117, 6:84, 8:69
as fuel, 5:82–83, 5:112–115
body waste as, 1:40–41, 2:24
collecting over water, 5:90–91
compressed, 5:32, 5:86–87, 5:102–103
cutting and welding with, 5:104–105
decomposition and, 5:110–111, 6:106
definition of, 5:26–27, 5:65
density, 5:78–79
dissolving in liquid, 5:88–89
exchanging, 3:86–87
flying by, 5:74–76
from gunpowder, 8:70–71
from rocket, 7:32
garbage and, 2:109
greenhouse effect and, 2:86–87
handling, 5:90–91
in atmosphere, 6:14
in space, 5:108–109
life and, 1:11
light and, 5:116–117
liquid, 5:100–101
made by chemical change, 5:38–40
plants and, 1:12, 1:82
separating from air, 5:52–53, 5:98–99
studying, 10:19
temperature and changes in, 5:30–33, 5:84–85, 5:100–101
transportation fumes, 2:97
uses of, 5:65, 5:96–97
see also **air; natural gas; ozone layer**
gas (fuel), see **gasoline**
gas balloon, see **hot-air balloon**
gasoline, 5:55, 5:94, *5:112,* 6:33, *8:65,* 8:71, 9:96
substitute for, 8:115
gasoline engine, 9:96–97
gas pipe, 9:54
gas pump, 9:100
gas stove, *4:10*
gas tank, 9:100
gas turbine, 9:95
gate (programming), 7:76-77, 7:88-89
gazelle, *3:106*
gear, *9:65,* 9:83, 9:84–86

gear shift, on bicycle, *9:87*
gecko, 3:96
Geiger counter, *2:105, 4:116*
gemstone, 6:56–57
General Sherman sequoia, 1:8–9
generator, 4:70–71, 4:106–107, 5:72, 8:93, 8:98, 8:100–101, 8:110
genus, 1:16
geodesic dome, 9:49
geologist, 6:24, 10:20
geostationary orbit, *7:36*
geostationary satellite, 8:50
geothermal energy, 4:75, 6:117, 8:112–113
germination, 1:94, 1:102–103

germination

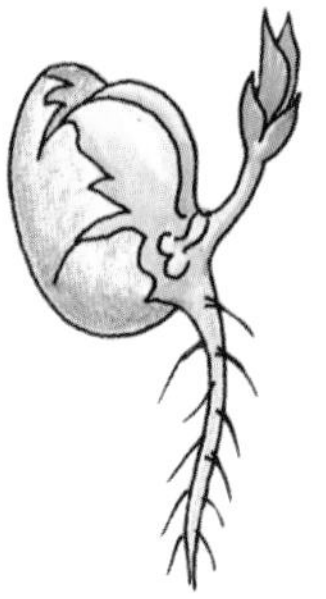

geyser, 6:23, *6:85*
g-force, 7:48, *7:51*
giant anteater, *3:89*
giant panda, 2:72, 2:75, *3:117*
giant tubeworm, 3:59
gibbous moon, 7:13
gigabyte, 7:88
gill, 1:29, 1:42, 3:66, *3:86*
gingko, 1:93
giraffe, *1:17*, 1:60, *3:74, 3:106*
girder, 9:26–27, 9:35
girder bridge, 9:35
glacier, 6:30, 6:34
Gladesville Bridge, *9:23*
gland, 1:51, 2:44–45
glass, 9:19
recycling, 2:112
gliding joint, 2:14
Global Positioning System, *8:50*
global warming, 2:86–87
globular cluster, 7:15
glucose, *2:45*, 5:68, 8:71
goat, 1:39
mountain, 3:105
goatsucker, *3:96*
goby, *3:66*
Goddard, Robert, *7:35*
goggles, *5:104*
gold, 6:52, 6:54, 6:55, *6:61*
golden swallow, *3:72*
gold salts, 6:50
gondola, 5:75
good luck plant, 1:106
gorilla, *1:17*, 2:75, *3:116*
GPS, *8:50*
grain elevator, *9:45*
gram, 10:33
Grand Canyon, 6:30
grandfather clock, 9:69
grand piano, 9:76
granite, 6:13, 6:24
grape, *1:111*
graphic design software, 7:110
graphic tablet, *7:95*
grass, 3:106
as food, 1:112–113
food chain and, 1:31
tundra, *1:70*
way of growing, 1:79
grasshopper, 3:29

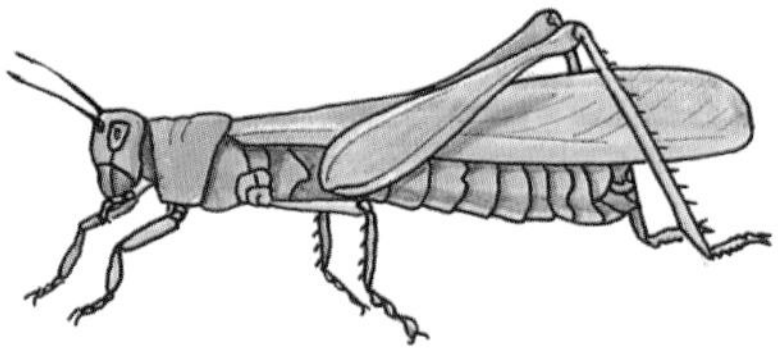

grasshopper

grassland, 1:78–79
invertebrates in, 3:38–39
overgrazing on, 2:89, 2:94, 2:95
vertebrates in, 3:106–107
gravitation, 7:30–31, 9:69–70
astronaut and, 7:48–49, 7:51
on moon, 7:12, 7:30
orbit and, 7:36
origins of solar system and, 6:10
tides and, 6:29
water and, 6:68–69
gravity, see **gravitation**
gray heron, 3:91
gray reef shark, *6:101*

gray whale, 3:95
grazing, 1:112, 2:89, 2:94, 2:95
grazing rotation, 1:117
Great Barrier Reef, 3:54–55
Great Bear, 7:14
Great Eastern, S.S. (ship), *8:32*
Great Stupa, *9:29*
Great Wall of China, *9:29*
green (color), 4:16–17, *8:46–47, 8:49*
green chameleon, *3:96*
greenhouse effect, 2:86–87
Greenland, 6:32–33
green plant, 1:37
  see also **plant**
green sea turtle, *3:65, 3:116*
grinding wheel, *9:113*
groundwater, 6:66, 6:73
ground wave, 8:35
ground wire, *4:59*
grouse, *3:73*
guard cell, *1:43*
gull, *3:83*
gulper eel, *3:64*
gulper fish, *3:85*
gunpowder, 7:32, 8:70
guy (wire), 9:39
gymnosperm, 1:93
gypsum, *5:22*
gyrocompass, 4:91

H

H_2O, 6:84
  see also **water**
habitat, 1:70, 2:71, 2:74, 3:30, 3:116
  see also specific habitats
hagfish, *3:64,* 3:66
hairdryer, 4:65
hairstreak butterfly, *1:12*
hairy spinifex grass, *1:79*
halogen light, 5:117
halophyte, 1:68
hammer
  of ear, 2:28–29
  on piano, 9:76
Hampton Court, *9:21*
handle bar, on bicycle, *9:87*
handset, on answering machine, *8:54*
hand washing, *2:56*
hard copy, *7:84*
hard disk, 7:84
hardware, computer, 7:84, 7:92–93
hare, *1:10, 2:82*
Hawaii, *6:27,* 8:109
Hawaiian land snail, *3:61*
hawk, *1:30, 3:72*
HDTV, 8:59
head, of insect, 3:24–25
head-mounted display, 7:111
hearing, *2:26,* 2:28, 3:92, 8:79
heart, 1:46–47
  human, 2:11, *2:16, 2:19,* 2:20–21

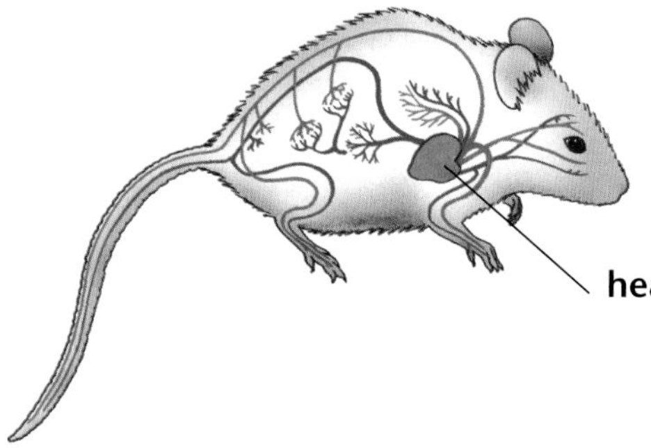

heat
  conducted, 6:89, 8:88–89
  for plant growth, 6:92
  from friction, 9:71, 9:113
  from water, 6:88–89, 6:117
  infrared, 4:23
  light and, 4:10–11, 4:70
  protecting building from, 9:58
  sensing, 2:32
  wire resistance and, 4:64–65, 4:112
  see also **temperature; temperature changes**
heat shield, 7:47
hedgehog, 3:89, *3:97*
height, human, 2:44

heliograph, 8:18
helium, 5:52, 5:78, 5:100, 5:108, 8:73
liquid, 5:101
hemoglobin, 2:18, 3:86, 3:104–105
herbaceous perennial, 1:109
herbivore, 1:30–31, 3:88
Hercules beetle, 3:58
hermaphrodite, 3:37
heron, 3:91
hertz, 4:115
hexagonal crystal, *5:22*
hibernation, 3:91
hibiscus flower, *1:95*
high-definition television, 8:59
high-level waste, 2:106
high pressure area, *6:39*
high tide, 6:29
Himalaya Mountains, 3:105, 6:19
hinge joint, 2:14
hippopotamus, *3:107,* 3:112
hive, honeybee, 3:27
hockey, 9:14
Hodgkin's disease, 2:59
hologram, 4:42–43
home, energy in, 8:67
home page, 7:108–109
honeybee, 3:27
honeydew, 3:42
honey possum, *1:99*
Hong Kong, *4:48–49, 5:116,* 9:42–43
hookworm, 3:14
Hoover Dam, *9:50*
hormone, 1:51, 2:44–45
horned viper, *3:100*
horse, 8:12
horse leech, *3:8*
horsetail, 1:64
host, 3:43
hot-air balloon, *5:8,* 5:74, *6:15*
hour, 10:33
house, *9:9,* 9:19
design of, 9:30–31
energy in, 2:114–115, 8:67
housefly, *2:56*
HTML, 7:100
Hubble Space Telescope, *7:22,* 7:28, 7:29, 7:46
human being, *3:65*
origins of, 6:11
human biologist, 10:21
human body, 2:8–61
amount of water in, 6:78
energy needs of, 8:74–75
floating by, 6:103
water needs of, 6:78–79
see also specific parts
human population, 2:65–66, 9:60
humidity, 5:107, 6:38
hummingbird, *3:72, 3:73, 3:109*

hummingbird

humus, 1:35, 1:85, 2:93
hunting, 2:74, 3:116
hurdler, *8:75*
hurricane, *5:73,* 6:47
hydraulic piston, 9:103
hydraulic power, 9:102–103
hydrocarbon, 2:97, 5:54–55, 5:57–59
hydrochloric acid, 5:24, 5:47
hydroelectricity, 2:98, 4:70, 6:116, 8:104–105, 9:50
hydrogen, 5:12, *5:17, 5:57,* 6:10
atom of, 8:73
in rocket fuel, 5:83
in space, 5:108
in water, 6:84
made from salt, 5:47
hygrometer, 6:40–41
hypertext, 7:109
hyphae, 1:29
hypothalamus, 2:44
Hz, 4:115

I

IAS, 7:93
ice, 5:106, 6:65, 6:84, 6:90–91, 8:69
  on Earth, 6:32–35
ice age, 6:33
iceberg, 6:35, 6:49, *6:90*

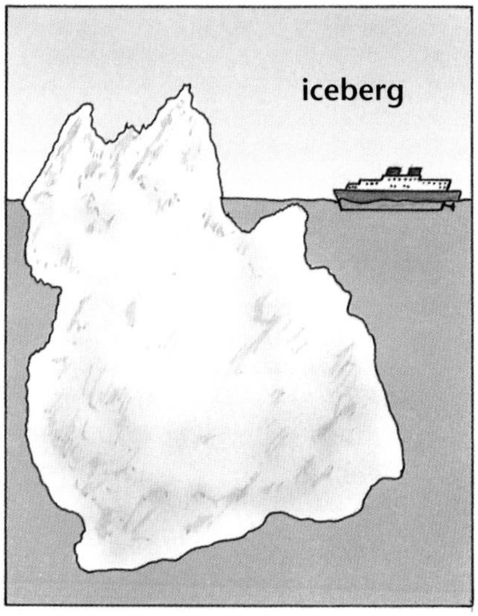

icebreaker ship, *6:32*
ice cream, 8:74
ice floe, 3:102
Iceland, 8:112
ice sheet, 6:32, 6:38
ichthyostega, 3:80
icicle, *6:85*
igneous rock, 6:24
Iguaçu Falls, *6:84*
iguana, *3:114*
illness, see **disease**
image
  eye and, 4:47
  reflection of, 4:28–29
  three-dimensional, 4:42–43, 4:46
immediate access store, 7:93
immune system, 2:50–53
imperial parrot, *3:117*
impulse turbine, 8:104–105
inch, 10:33
inch-pound system, 7:72
incisor, 3:88–89
inclined plane, 9:65, 9:78–79
India, 2:74, 6:18, *6:43, 6:74*
Indian elephant, *1:60, 3:74*
Indian pangolin, *3:97*
Indians, of Peru, 3:104
indicator, 5:24–25
indigestion, 5:25
Indonesia, *6:77*
Indus River dolphin, *3:117*
inert gas, 5:116
inertia, 5:65, 8:86, 9:69
infection, *1:56*
infrared film, 4:23
infrared lamp, *4:117*
infrared photography, 7:42
infrared ray, 4:22–23, 4:116–117
infrared telescope, 7:29
infrared wave, 8:80–81
ingot, 5:51
inhaling, 1:42, 2:16–17, 5:92
inkjet printer, 7:102
inner core (Earth), 6:12–13, 6:17
inner ear, *2:26*, 2:28
inorganic materials, 1:86
input, 7:82, *7:92–93*
input device, 7:85, 7:94–95
insect, 3:22–29
  body of, 3:24–25
  breathing, 1:43
  camouflage, 1:57
  decomposition and, 1:35
  eaten by plant, *1:11*, 1:81
  eye of, 4:47
  helpful, 3:57
  muscle of, *1:48*
  pests, 3:56–57
  pollination by, 1:98
  social, 3:26–27
  warning color, 1:57
  wing of, *1:48*
insect eater, 3:89
insectivore, 3:89

insoluble substance, 5:18, 6:105
insulation, 4:58–59, 9:58–59
insulator, 4:50–51, 8:89, 9:58
insulin, *2:45*
integrated circuit, 7:86, 7:91, *8:42,* 8:44
intelligent agent, 8:61
Intelstat VIII-A (satellite), *8:51*
intensive agriculture, 2:88–90, 2:90
interference, signal, see **signal**
interglacial period, 6:33
internal combustion engine, 9:96–97
international Morse code, 8:17
International Space Station, 7:55
International Telecommunications Satellite Organization, *8:51*
Internet, 7:65, 7:107, 8:60
  see also **World Wide Web**
interstellar space, 7:61
intestine
  large, 2:24
  small, 1:38–39, 2:19, *2:23*
invertebrate, 3:8–61
  by place
    coral reefs, 3:54–55
    deserts, 3:44–45
    freshwater habitats, 3:34–36
    grasslands, 3:36–37
    oceans, 3:46–51
    seashores, 3:52–53
    tropical rain forest, 3:42–43
    woodlands, 3:40–41
  definition of, 3:8–9
  endangered, 3:60–61
  extraordinary, 3:58–59
  watching and learning about, 3:30–33
  see also specific types
involuntary muscle, 2:15
Io, 7:58
ion, 5:17, 5:19
ionosphere, 4:87, 5:71, 6:14–15, 8:35
ipecac, 1:114
Ireland, *8:114*
iridium, 6:55
iris, of eye, *2:34*
iron (metal), 6:54, *6:61,* 9:42, 10:17
  atom of, 5:12–13
  construction with, 9:26
  in Earth, 6:13, 6:51
  in magnet, 4:80
  rusting of, 5:40, 5:60, 5:69, 6:110–111, 9:26
  steel from, 5:44, 8:68
iron ore, 5:44, 6:52
iron ore mine, *6:52, 6:53*
iron oxide, 5:44, 6:110–111
irrigation, 6:77, *6:117*
island, 6:13
  animals of, 3:114–115
isometric crystal, *5:22*
ivory-billed woodpecker, *3:117*
ivy, *1:15*

J

jacana, *3:113*
jack, 9:81
jacket (structure), 9:40
jackscrew, 9:81
Jackson, Charles, 8:16
jaguar, *1:17*
Japan, 6:21, 6:23
jaundice, *4:116*
jaw, 3:88
jellyfish, *3:8,* 3:12–13, 3:46, 3:48–49, *6:78*

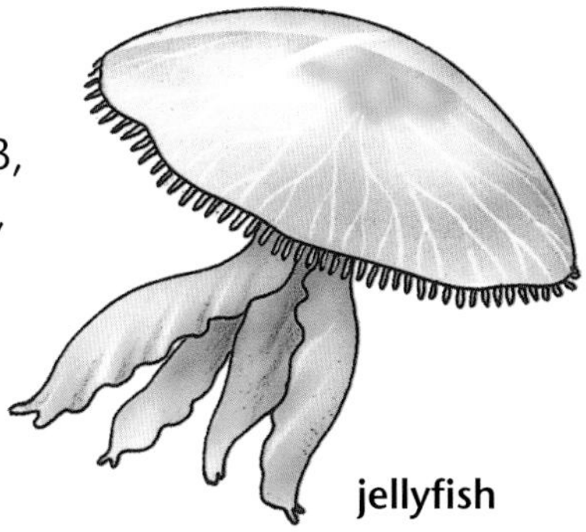

jellyfish

jerboa, *3:100*
jet, of water, 6:114–115
jet aircraft, *6:15*
John F. Kennedy Space Center, *7:9*
joint, 1:48
  arthropod, 3:22
  human, 2:14
joystick, *7:94*
Jupiter, 7:20–23, 7:30, 7:58, *7:60*

K

kangaroo, *3:79, 3:90*
Kariba Dam, *6:116*
Keck telescopes, 4:31, 7:26–27
kelp, *1:25*
Kennedy Space Center, *7:9*
Kenya, *8:67*
kerosene, 5:55
key, *5:8*
piano, 9:76
telegraph, 8:20
keyboard
calculator, *7:83*
computer, 7:84–85, *7:92*
musical, *7:87, 9:76*
keystone, 9:35
kidney, 1:40, 2:19, 2:24–25
kidney machine, 2:25
killer whale, *2:83*
kiln, 9:20
kilogram, 10:33
kilometer, 7:73, 10:33
kindling temperature, 5:94
kinetic energy, 8:68–69, 8:84, 8:86, 8:91, 8:98, 8:104, 9:90
kingdom, 1:12, 1:16
kingfisher, *3:65*
king penguin, *3:110*
king termite, 3:26
Kiruna, Sweden, 6:52
kite, *5:77*
knowledge, in science, 10:12, 10:26
koala, *2:72*

kombu, *1:25*
Komodo dragon, 2:75
krypton, 5:117

L

laboratory, *10:9,* 10:24
safety in, 10:38–39
ladybug, 3:57
lake, *9:61*
animals in, 3:112
lamppost, *9:9*
lamprey, *3:64,* 3:66
LAN, 7:107
lander, 7:59
landfill, 5:111–112
Landsat (satellite), 7:42–43
land snail, *3:9, 3:61*
laptop computer, 7:91
large intestine, 2:24
larvae, 3:15, 3:28, 3:34, 3:41, *3:47,* 3:50
laser, 4:40–45, 6:56, 7:103
in bar code reader, 7:105
in communication, 8:57, 8:58
laser printer, 7:103
lateral line, 3:92
latex, 5:58–59
lathe, *9:112*
latitude, lines of, 6:42
lattice structure, 9:38–39
launching system, 7:46
launch vehicle, 7:34
lava, 6:23, *6:24*
lava quarry, *2:68*
lawn sprinkler, 6:115
lead, *5:17, 5:61,* 6:33, 6:52, *6:61*
lead-free gasoline, *2:117*
leaf, 1:88–89, *1:93*
essential oil, 1:76
falling, 1:73
leafy liverwort, *1:64*
Leaning Tower of Pisa, *9:33*
leech, 3:15
lemur, 3:115
length, *7:72*
lens, 4:30–35
eye, 2:34–35
telescope, 7:26
leopard, *1:17, 1:39, 3:117*

leopard seal, *2:83*
lettuce, *6:79*
leukemia, 2:59
lever, 9:65, 9:67, 9:72–77
levitation, magnetic, 4:108–110
liana, 1:75
library database, 7:106
lichen, 1:29
life, 10:14
  cells and, 1:9
  classification of, 1:12–17
  definition of, 1:11
  development of, 1:60–61
  origins on Earth, 6:10
  water and, 6:65
life cycle
  crustacean, 3:37, 3:50
  earthworm, 3:37
  echinoderm, 3:51
  fluke, 3:15
  frog, 3:68–69
  insect, 3:28–29
  jellyfish, 3:49
  octopus, 3:51
  scorpion, 3:36
  snail, 3:37
  spider, 3:36
  sponge, 3:48–49
life cycle kit, 3:29
life expectancy, 2:66
life-support system, for astronaut, 7:44
lift (airplane), 5:76-77, 9:104
ligament, 2:13
light, 4:8–47
  artificial, 4:9
  communicating with, 8:18–19, 8:56–57
  direction of travel, 4:12–13
  emission, 4:10–11, 4:25, 4:40
  fluorescent, 4:10–11, 4:14
  gas and, 5:116–117
  heat and, 4:10–11, 4:70
  natural, 4:8
  scattered, 4:38–39
  sources of, 4:8, 4:10, 4:24–25
  speed of, 4:36–37, 6:45, 7:31, 8:50, 8:81
  visible, *8:80*
  wavelength of, 4:12, 4:16
  wave of, 4:12, 4:16, 8:46, 8:80–81
  see also **color; laser; reflection; refraction**
light bulb, 4:52, 4:53, 4:64, 5:116–117
lighthouse, *8:19,* 9:44
lightning, 4:49, 4:57, 6:44, 8:13, 8:98
light show, *4:41*
light-year, 7:31, 8:81
lignite, 8:96–97
lily, *1:65,* 1:66
lime, 6:108
limescale, 6:108
limestone, 5:45, 6:18, 6:108
limpet, 3:52
linear electric motor, 4:111
lion, *1:17,* 1:31, *3:90*
lion tamarin, 2:72–73
liquid, 5:9, 5:26–27, 5:65, 8:68–69
  density of, 6:107
  distilling, 5:98
  gas in, 5:88–89
  measuring, *10:35*
  temperature and changes in, 5:28–32
  water as, 6:65, 6:84
  see also **water**
liquid gas, 5:52, 5:100–101
liquid helium, 5:101
liquid nitrogen, 5:53, 5:99, 5:101
liquid oxygen, 5:53, 5:101
liquid plastic foam, 9:58
LISP (computer language), 7:100
litmus paper, 5:25
Little Bear (constellation), 7:14
liver, 2:19
liverwort, *1:64, 1:90*
lizard, *3:65,* 3:70, *3:79, 3:101*
load, 9:72
lobster, 3:46–47
local area network, 7:107
locust, *1:44, 3:9,* 3:29, *3:44,* 3:56–57
lodestone, 4:91
log cabin, *9:18*

life cycle of a frog

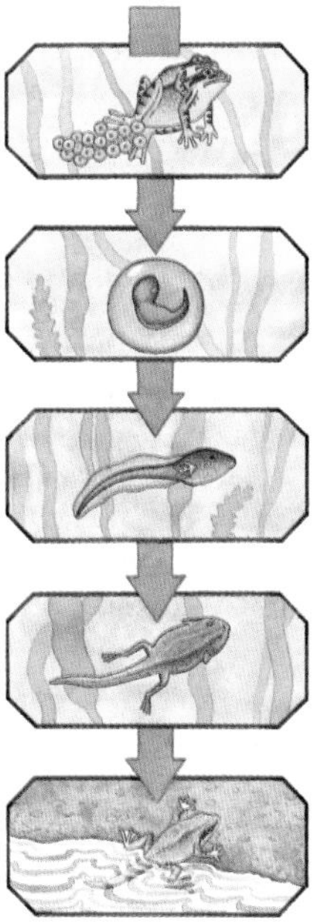

loggerhead turtle, *3:111*
logic, 7:74–75
Logo (computer language), 7:100
London, *9:46*
long-distance call, 8:28
long-spined urchin, *3:9*
loudspeaker, 4:101
Louisiana pearlshell, *3:61*
louse, wood, 3:22, 3:33, 3:37
low-level waste, 2:106
low pressure area, *6:39*
low tide, 6:29
lubrication, 9:71
Lucid, Shannon, 7:54
lugworm, *3:53*
lumber company, *1:117*
"lunar," 7:12
lunar module, 7:56
lunar roving vehicle, *7:57*
lung, 1:42, 2:16–17, 3:68, 3:87, 6:103
lungfish, 3:67
lycophyte, 1:64
lymphocyte, 2:50
lynx spider, *1:39*

M

macaque, *5:26*
macaw, *3:73, 3:108*
machine, 9:63–117
  forces and, 9:68–69
  friction in, 9:70–71
  perpetual motion, 9:66
  see also **simple machines**
machine tool, 9:112–113
macrophage, 2:50
Madagascar, 3:115
Magellan (space probe), 7:58
Magellanic Clouds, 7:19
magenta, *4:17*
maglev train, *4:79,* 4:110–111
magma, 6:22, 6:23, *6:24*
magnesium, 6:50
magnet, 4:78–117
  bar, *4:81,* 4:85, 4:86
  care of, 4:89
  cutting in half, 4:89
  making, 4:88
  permanent, 4:80
  poles, 4:81–82, 4:98
  shapes, 4:81
  strength, 4:83, 4:93
  see also **electromagnet**
magnetic compass, see **compass, magnetic**
magnetic field, 4:78, 4:84–85, *4:115*
  of Earth, 4:86–87
magnetic levitation, 4:108–110
magnetic levitation vehicle, 4:110
magnetic poles
  on Earth, 4:86
  on magnet, 4:81–82, 4:98
magnetic puppet theater, 10:25
magnetism, 4:78–79
  see also **magnet**
magnification, 10:18
magnifying glass, *8:43, 8:49,* 8:56
mahogany, *1:74*
mainframe computer, 7:90–91
mainspring, 9:84
malaria, 1:55, 2:54, *2:55,* 3:56
Malaysia, *6:95*
malignant tumor, 2:59
mallow, *1:94*
mammal, 1:16, 2:46, *3:65,* 3:74–75
  blood in, 1:46
  development through time, 1:60
  eating by, 3:88–89
  ocean, 3:110–111
  pollination and, *1:99*
  waste, *1:40*
Mammalia, *3:65*
mammoth, *1:60*
manganese, 6:51, 6:54, *6:61*
mangrove swamp, 1:69
mangrove tree, *1:41,* 1:69
mantle (Earth), 6:12–13, 6:17, 6:19, 6:22
manual transmission, 9:98
manufacturing, 6:49, *6:76,* 7:114

manzanita shrub, *1:76*
mapacu, *1:74*
maple, *1:73*
maple seed, *1:100*
marble, *9:18*
Marconi, Guglielmo, 8:34
Mariana Trench, *6:27*
marine biologist, 10:21
marine fish, see **saltwater fish**
marine iguana, *3:114*
marine otter, 2:75
maritime compass, 4:91
market, *2:60*
marlin, *3:64*
marrow, 2:12–13
Mars, *7:20–23*, *7:59*, 7:115
marsh, 1:68
marsh fern, *1:64*
marsh horsetail, *1:64*
marsh samphire, 1:68
marsh warbler, *3:73*
Mars Pathfinder, 7:59
Mars Polar Lander, 7:59
Mars Sojourner Rover, 7:59
marsupial, 3:74–75
martin, *3:72*
mask
for silicon chip, 8:45
shadow, *8:49*
mass, 5:65, 10:32, 10:36
mass production, 9:114
mast, 9:39
materials
for science activities, 10:30–31
survey of, 6:58–60
materials, construction, 9:8, 9:12–13, 9:18–27
brick, 9:20–21
cement, 9:22–23
concrete, see **concrete**
glass, 9:19
insulation, 9:58–59
iron, 9:26, 9:42
steel, see **steel**
stone, 9:18
wood, 9:18
mat foundation, *9:32*
matter, 4:24, 5:9, 5:65, 7:30
building blocks of, 5:10–11

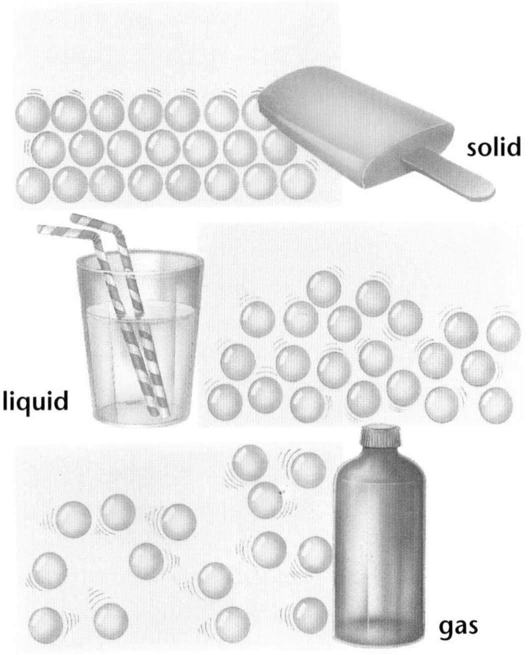

Mauna Loa, 6:23
mayfly, *3:34*
measurement, 7:72–73, 10:32–37
measuring cup, *7:72*
meat eater, 3:89
mechanical advantage, 9:73, 9:81
mechanical energy, 9:90
medicine, 2:59
infrared rays in, 4:23
laser use in, 4:41
plants in, 1:114–115
Mediterranean monk seal, *3:116*
Mediterranean Sea, 6:29
megabyte, 7:88
megaphone, 8:11
melanin, 4:21
melting, 5:44–45, 5:104–105, 6:91
melting point, 5:28
membrane
ameba, 1:23
bacteria, *1:27*
cell, 1:18–19
ear, 2:28
osmosis and, 6:94

memory, computer, 7:82, 7:96–97
memory cell, 7:97
memory chip, 7:97
Mercalli scale, 6:21
mercury (metal), 5:81, 6:54
Mercury (planet), 7:20–23
mercury barometer, 5:81
mesopause, 6:14–15
mesosphere, 5:71, 6:14–15
message, to and from brain, 3:77
  see also **communication; signal**
metal, *5:8*, 6:54–55
  as conductor, 4:59
  coatings of, 5:48–49
  corrosion, 6:110–111
  cutting and welding, 5:104–105
  formation of, 6:52
  from ocean, 6:50, 6:51
  magnetic versus nonmagnetic, 4:80, 4:95
  melting, 5:44–45
  mining for, 6:54
  moving with magnet, *4:78*, 4:95
  properties, 5:15
  recycled, 2:112, 4:94
  see also specific metals
metal detector, 4:102–103
metal plate, 9:55
metamorphic rock, 6:24–25
metamorphosis, 3:28
meteor, 7:20, 7:24
meteorite, 7:24
meteorologist, 6:40, 10:20
meter, 10:33
methane, 2:109, 5:110–111, 5:114–115, 8:114, 8:116–117
metric system, 7:72
Mexican worm lizard, *3:79*
microbe, 2:48–49
microbiologist, 10:21
microcomputer, 7:91
  see also **computer**
microgravity, 7:48
micrometer, 7:73
microorganism, 2:48
microphone, 8:25, *8:46*
microprocessor, 7:86, 8:44
microscope, *1:8*, 1:20, 5:9, 8:68, 10:18
  electron, 5:10, 10:18–19
microwave, 4:116–117, 8:27, 8:50
microwave dish, *4:117*
microwave oven, *4:117*, *7:87*
middle ear, 2:28–29
migration, 3:94–95
mile, 10:33
milk, *6:79*
Milky Way Galaxy, 7:18
millet, 1:112
millimeter, 10:33
milling tool, *9:113*
millipede, 3:22
mimosa plant, 1:80
mine, 6:12, *6:52*, 6:53
mineral, 2:12, *5:8*, 6:24
  as natural resource, 6:52, 6:61
  in diet, 2:22
  in drinking water, 6:80, 6:92
  in ocean, 6:50, 6:51

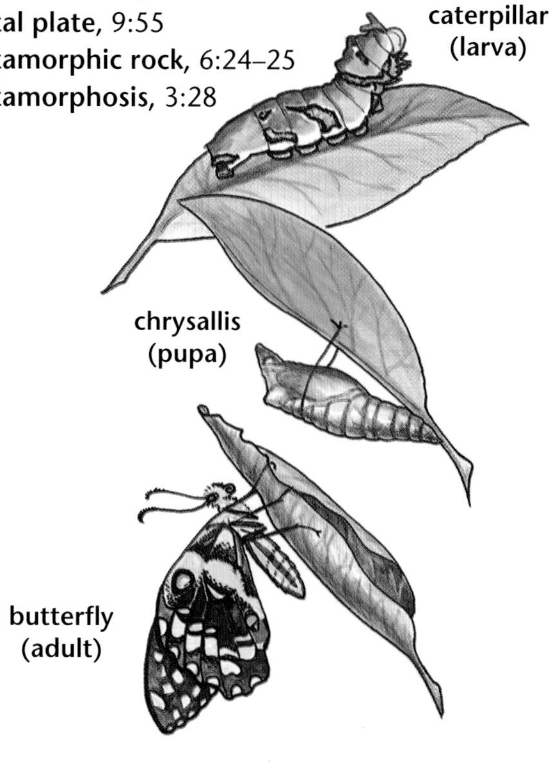

feldspar

mineral wool fiber, *9:58*
minicomputer, 7:91
mining, *2:64, 2:68*
Earth, 6:53
ocean, 6:51
minute, 10:33
Mir (space station), 7:54
mirage, *4:27*
mirror, 4:28–31, 7:26
heliograph, 8:18
solar energy, 8:107
mission control, 7:41, *7:113*
mission specialist, 7:50
mitochondria, 1:18–19
mixture, 5:20–21
MLV, 4:110
mobile telephone, 8:52
modem, *7:84,* 7:105, 8:9, 8:60
moisture, 9:56–57
Mojave Desert, 8:107, 8:109
molar, 3:88–89
mold, *1:28*
mole (animal), *3:78*
molecule, 5:16, *5:27,* 8:68
in gas, 5:85
in melting ice, 5:29
water, 6:84, 6:96, 6:97

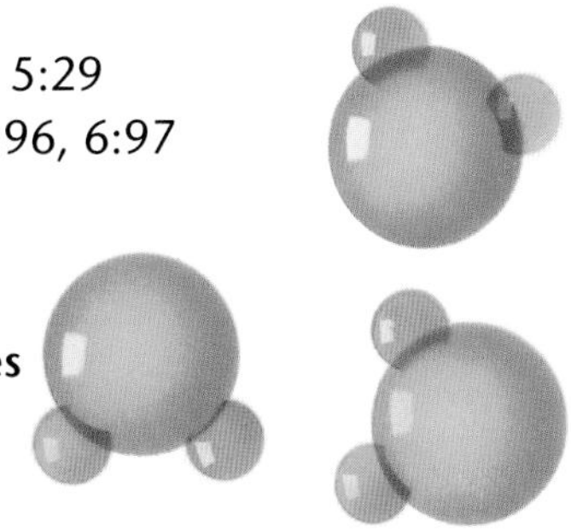

water molecules

Mollusca, 3:9
mollusk, 3:9, 3:20–21
molten rock, 6:13, 6:17
molting, 3:50
moment magnitude scale, 6:21
moneran, 1:13
monitor (computer), 7:84–85, *7:92*
monkey, 3:108, *5:26, 10:14*
monoclinic crystal, *5:22*
monomer, *5:57*
monotreme, 3:74–75
Monterey flatworm, *3:8*
moon, 7:12–13
gravity on, 7:12, 7:30
tides and, 6:29
travel to, 7:56–57, 7:115
moon buggy, *7:57*
moraine, 6:34
morning star, 7:22
Morse, Samuel, 8:16
Morse code, 8:16–19, 8:21, 8:22, 8:34
mortar, 9:22
mosquito, 2:54, 3:43
moss, *1:12, 1:64,* 1:90, 1:107
moth, 3:28, 3:57
motion, *9:68*
motor, electric, 4:104–105, 4:111, 9:108–109
mountain, 3:104–105
climate, 6:43
formation, 6:18–19
road on, 9:78–79

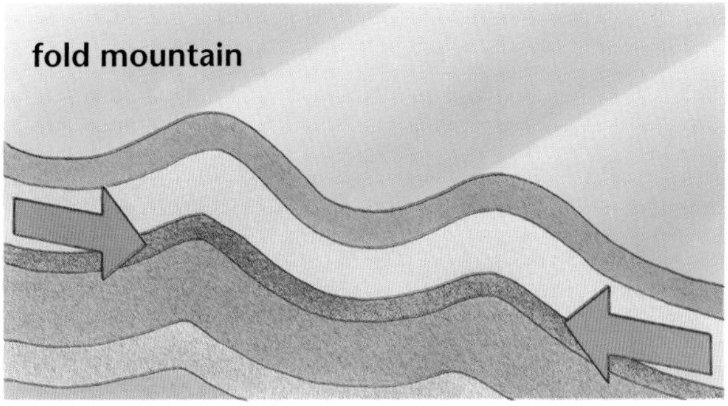

mountain goat, 3:105
mountain gorilla, 2:75, *3:116*
Mount Etna, *6:23*
Mount Everest, 6:18
Mount Fuji, 6:23
Mount Whaleback, Australia, *6:52*
mouse, *1:30,* 2:70–71, *3:65, 3:100*
as prey, *1:50*
blood of, *1:47*
mouse, computer, 7:85, *7:92, 7:95*
mouthpiece, telephone, 8:25
movement, 1:48–51
ameba, 1:23
involuntary, 1:50
of human body, 2:9, 2:14, 2:41–43
voluntary, 1:50
mucus, 3:68

mudskipper, 1:42
multimedia program, *7:99*
multimeter, 4:62
multiplexer, 8:28–29
multiplication, *7:70*, *7:81*
multistage flash distillation, 6:49
multistage rocket, *7:34*
muscle, 1:48, 1:50
  human, 2:11, 2:15, 2:41
muscle cell, 1:20–21, 2:11
mushroom, 1:13, *1:15*, 1:28–29, 1:85
mussel, 3:20–21, 3:52
Myxini, *3:64*

N

Namib Desert, 1:80, *6:85*, 6:93
Namib lizard, *3:101*
naphtha, 5:55
national park, 2:80
natural fertilizer, 6:92
natural gas, 4:74, *5:64–65*, 5:94, 5:113–115, *6:61*, 8:67
naturalist, 3:30–31
natural resources, 2:65, 2:68, 6:52–57
  ocean, 6:50–51
  renewable versus nonrenewable, 6:60–61
natural science, 10:10
natural selection, 1:66
nature, 10:12, 10:14
nautilus shell, 9:25
navel, 2:47
Navstar (satellite), *8:50*
neap tide, 6:29
Near Earth Asteroid Rendezvous (spacecraft), 7:58
nebula, 6:10, 7:16
nectar, 1:98, 3:27
needle, *1:93*
needle-tailed swift, 3:95
negative charge, 4:56
nekton, 3:46
Nelson, Admiral Horatio, 8:15
Nematoda, *3:8*, 3:14
Nemertea, 3:8, 3:14
neon, 5:52, 5:117
Nepalese swift, 3:105
Neptune, 7:20–23, 7:61
nerve, 3:77
nerve cell, 1:20, 2:10–11, 2:40
nerve ending, *2:26*
nervous system, 1:51, 3:77
  human, 2:9, 2:40
nest, *3:73*, 9:8
net, fishing, *6:50*
network
  communication, 8:61
  computer, 7:107
neutralization, 5:25
neutron, 5:10–13, 8:73

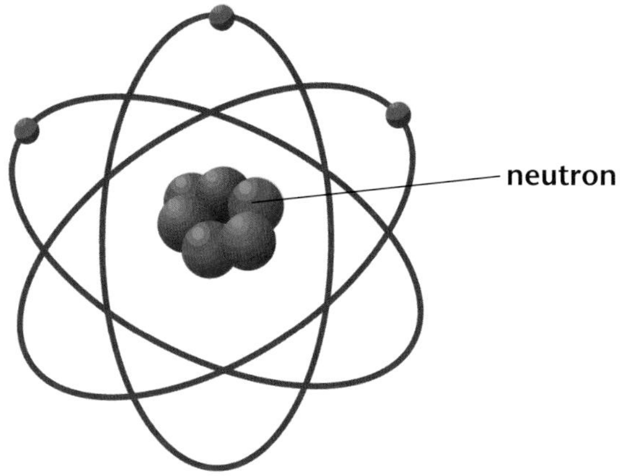

neutron star, 7:16
Newcastle University, *9:49*
new moon, 7:13
newsgroup, 7:107, 8:60
newspaper, 8:22, 8:23
news service, 8:23
newt, *3:64*
Newton, Isaac, 6:114
New York City, 9:42
New Zealand, 3:114
Next Generation Space Telescope, 7:29
NGST (telescope), 7:29
nickel, 4:80, 6:13, 6:51, *6:61*
nightjar, *3:96*

Nile crocodile, *3:71*
Nile River, *9:35*
nitrate, 5:96
nitric acid, 2:98
nitrogen, *5:12*, 6:14
in air, 5:52, 5:68
liquid, 5:53, 5:99, 5:101
uses for, 5:96
nitrogen oxide, 2:97
nodule, ocean, 6:51
noise, 8:13, 8:40, 8:78–79
nonbiodegradable material, 2:111
nonmagnetic material, 4:80
nonmetal, 5:14–15
nonrenewable resource, 6:60–61
nonrenewable source of energy, 8:67, 8:92
nonvascular plant, 1:90
nori, 6:50
north, finding, 4:91
Northern Hemisphere, *6:36–37*
northern lights, see **aurora**
north magnetic pole (Earth), 4:86
North Pole (Earth), 2:82, 4:86, 6:32, 6:36–37, 7:73
north pole, of magnet, 4:81, 4:82, 4:96
North Star, 4:90, 7:14
Norway maple, *1:73*
Norway spruce, *1:93, 1:96*
nose, *2:26*, 2:31
notebook computer, 7:91
NOT gate, 7:88–89
nozzle, *9:101*
nuclear change, 5:60–61
nuclear dump, 2:107

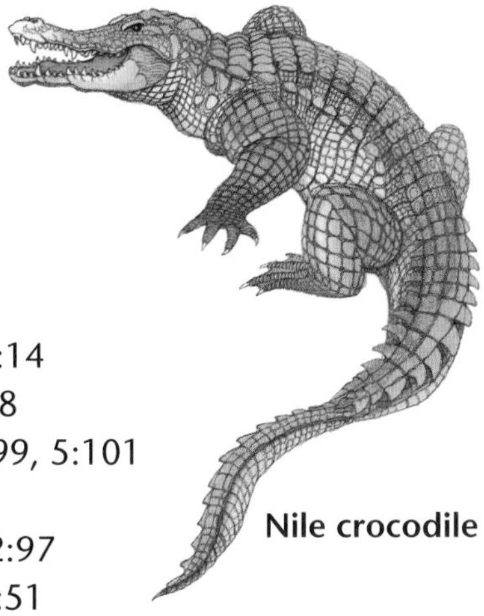
Nile crocodile

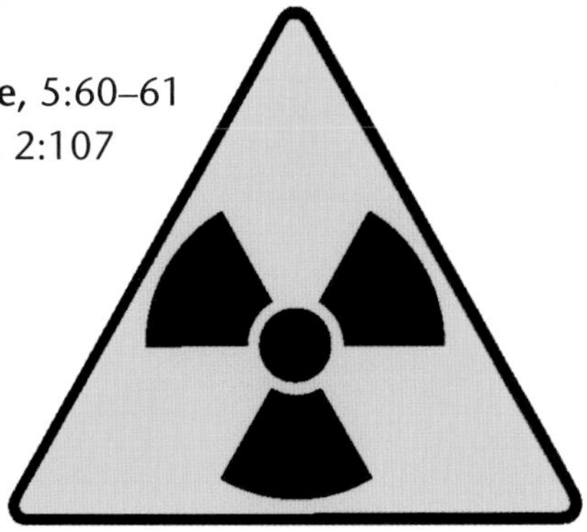
international radiation symbol

nuclear energy, 8:73, 8:102–103
fission, 8:73, 8:102
fusion, 5:109, 8:73, 8:95, 8:102
pollution and, 2:99, 2:104–107
see also **nuclear power station**
nuclear explosion, *8:73*
nuclear physicist, 10:21
nuclear power station, 4:70, 8:73, 8:103
nuclear processing plant, *2:107*
nuclear reaction, 6:11
nuclear waste, 2:105–107
nucleoid, *1:27*
nucleus, of atom, 4:24, 5:10–11, 5:60, 8:73
nucleus, of cell, 1:18–19, 1:20–21, 2:10
in ameba, 1:23
nut (mechanical part), 9:80
nutrient, 1:32, 1:33, 2:19, 2:88, 3:16
in seed, 6:92
water as, 6:78–81
nymph, 3:29, *3:44*

O

oak, *1:65*
oak apple, 3:41
oak gall, 3:41
observation, 10:12
observation cell, 3:35
observation satellite, 7:42
ocean, 6:26–29
as source of energy, 8:110–111
bottom of, 6:27, 6:51
cables on floor of, 8:32, 8:33
erosion by, 6:30, 6:31
food chain in, 1:31
formation of, 6:26
invertebrates in, 3:46–55
movement of, 6:28–29, 6:98–99
oil platforms in, 9:40–41
percentage of Earth's surface, 6:9, 6:26
resources from, 6:50–51
salt from, 6:48–49
vertebrates in, 3:110–111

ozone layer, 2:84, 2:86, 5:70, 6:14–15

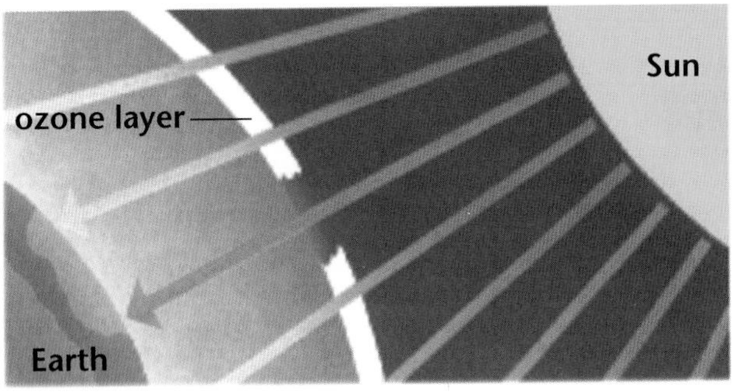

P

Pacific blue star, *3:9*
Pacific Ocean, 6:21, *6:27, 7:43*
Pacific yew, 2:59
paddle worm, *3:47*
pager, 8:52
pain, 3:77
palace, *9:21*, 9:28
pallid sturgeon, *3:117*
palmtop computer, 7:91
pampas grass, *1:79*
pancreas, *2:45*
panda, 2:72, 2:75, *3:90, 3:117*
Pangaea, *6:16*
paper, 5:94
  recycling, 2:112–113
papyrus, *1:67*
paramecium, *1:19*, 1:22
parasite, 1:28, 1:54–55, 3:14, 3:43
park, 2:80, *2:117*
parrot, *3:108, 3:109, 3:117*

parrots

Pascal (computer language), 7:100
passion flower, *1:65*
paving truck, *9:52*
payload, 7:47
payload specialist, 7:50
PDA, 7:91
peacock, *1:17*
peanut, *1:110*
pearlshell, *3:61*
peat, 8:96–97, *8:114*
peat moss, *1:64*
peccary, *3:90*
pedal
  bicycle, *9:87*
  piano, 9:76–77
pelagic sea snake, *3:111*
pelican, *1:36*
pendulum, 8:82, 9:84
pendulum clock, 9:84
penguin, *1:44, 2:83, 3:73*, 3:103, 3:110–111
perennial, 1:109
periodic table of the elements, 5:14
periosteum, 2:12–13
periscope, 4:29
periwinkle, rosy, 2:59
perpetual motion, 9:66
personal computer, 7:91
personal digital assistant, 7:91
personal identification number, 7:104
Peru, 3:104
pest, 3:56–57
pesticide, 2:70–71, 2:90
pet, and health, *2:56*
Petawatt laser, 4:41
petroleum, *6:61, 8:65*, 8:67
  see also **oil**
phagocyte, 2:50–51
pharmacist, 10:21
phase, moon, 7:12
pheasant, *3:83*
Philippine eagle, 2:75
phloem, 1:47
pH number, 5:24
phosphor, 8:48, *8:49*
photodegradable plastic, 2:111

photoelectric effect, *4:116*
photography, 7:41–42, 7:110
  infrared, 4:22–23
  see also **camera**
photon, 4:25, 4:40
photosynthesis, 1:37, 1:43, 1:84
photovoltaic cell, 8:107
phylum, 1:16, 3:8

penguins

giant panda

lizard

physical change, 5:36
physical chemist, 10:21
physical science, 10:11
physicist, 10:20
physics, 10:20
phytoplankton, 3:46
piano, 9:76–77
pier foundation, *9:32*
pig, *1:17*
pile foundation, *9:32*
pillar, *9:9*
piloted spacecraft, 7:44
pine tree, *1:15, 1:65*
PIN number, 7:104
pin-tailed sandgrouse, *3:101*
pinwheel, 5:72
pipeline, 8:93
pistol shrimp, 3:59
piston, 8:91, *9:92,* 9:96–97, 9:103, 10:17
piston engine, 9:96–97
pitch, 9:81
pitcher plant, 1:81
pitfall trap, 3:38–39
pituitary gland, 1:51, 2:44–45
pivot joint, 2:14
pixel, 7:110
placenta, 2:46–47
placental, 3:74–75
placer deposit, 6:52
plan, building, 9:31
plane (vehicle), see **airplane**
plane, inclined, see **inclined plane**
plane mirror, 4:28
planet, 6:9, 7:9, 7:20–23
  origins of, 6:11
plankton, 1:24, 1:31, 3:35, 3:46
plant, 1:63–117
  air and, 1:43, 5:68
  as parasite, 1:55
  by place
    chaparral, 1:76–77
    dry places, 1:70–71
    forest, 1:72–73
    grassland, 1:78–79
    rain forest, 1:74–75, 2:78–81
    wet places, 1:66–69
  cell of, 1:9, 1:21, 1:84
  classification, 1:12, 1:16, 1:64–65
  decomposition and, 1:32–35
  defenses by, 1:56
  development through time, 1:59, 1:61
  endangered species, 1:116–117, 2:72
  energy storage by, 8:71
  extraordinary, 1:80–81
  food from, 1:110–113
  food production by, 1:12, 1:37, 1:84
  growth of, 1:82–87
  in food chain, 1:30–31
  medicine from, 1:114–115
  parts of, 1:88–89

protecting, 2:76–77
reproduction by, 1:94–107
sap of, 1:47
seed, 1:92–93
spore, 1:90–91
waste, 1:41
water cycle and, 6:66–67
water in, 6:92–95
winter and, 1:108–109
see also **agriculture**; specific plants

plant eater, 3:88, 3:89
plasma, 2:18
plastic, 4:19, 4:59, 5:56–57
as building material, 9:19, 9:58
recycling, 2:111
platinum, 6:52, 6:55
Platyhelminthes, 3:8, 3:15
platypus, *3:75*
playground, *2:61*
Pleiades (star cluster), 7:15
Pleistocene Ice Age, 6:33
plover, *3:96*
Pluto, 7:20–21, 7:23
pneumatic tire, *9:86*
pneumonia, *1:26*, 1:55
poacher, 2:74
poison, *1:28*, 1:114, *3:97*
polar bear, 2:75, *2:82*, *3:96*, 3:102
polar orbit, *7:36*
polar region animals, 3:102–103
pole (Earth), see **North Pole**; **South Pole**
poles, magnetic, see **magnetic poles**
polestar, 7:14
pollen, 1:53, 3:27
pollination, 1:98–99
pollution, 3:116
air, 2:96–99, *2:117*, 6:61
evidence of, in ice, 6:33
water, 2:100–103, *2:116*, 6:61, 6:82
see also **waste**
polyethylene, 5:57
Polykov, Valery, 7:54
polymer, 5:57
polyp
coral, 3:13, 3:54
jellyfish, 3:48–49
polytrichum moss, *1:64*
pond skater, *3:34*
Pont du Gard, *9:34*
Pony Express, 8:12
poppy, *1:92*, *2:82*
population, human, 2:65–66, 9:60
porcupine, *3:97*
porcupine fish, *3:67*
pore
skin, 2:33
sponge, 3:11
Porifera, 3:8, 3:10
porous material, 9:15
portable computer, 7:91
portable radio, 8:42
portable telephone, *8:8*
positive charge, 4:56
possum, *1:99*
potato, 1:106, *6:79*
potential energy, 8:76–77, 8:84, 9:90
pound, 10:32, 10:33
power, 9:67
power pool, 8:99

power station, 4:58, 4:70–71, *8:65,* 8:83
hydroelectric, 8:104–105
nuclear, 8:73, 8:102–103
solar, 8:107
tidal, 8:110–111
power steering, 9:98
prairie, 1:78
precious metal, 6:55
precipitation, 6:38
predator, 3:96
pregnancy, 2:46–47
prehistoric times, 3:80–81
pre-set tuning, 8:39
press brake, *9:112*
pressure, 5:84, 6:91, 9:50, 9:104
see also **air pressure**
prestressed concrete, 9:23
prey, 3:96

prickly pear flower, *3:45*
printer, 7:84, *7:92,* 7:102–103
printing plant, 6:76
printing plate, 9:111
printing press, 9:110–111
prism, 4:14–15
problem-solving, 7:100, 10:9, 10:13
see also **calculation**
proboscis, 3:14
program, see **computer program**
programmer, 7:100
programming language, 7:100–101
Project Tiger, 2:74
prokaryote, 1:13
prominence (sun), 7:11
propane, 5:86, 5:112
propeller, 9:94, 9:104
property
of element, 5:15
of materials, 6:58–59, 9:12
protective clothing, 9:14
protective glasses, *4:21*
protein, 2:22, 2:60, 5:96, 8:75
in cells, 1:19
in food, 1:38
protist, 1:13, 1:22, 2:48, 2:54–55
proton, 5:10–13, 8:73
protonema, *1:107*
protozoan, 1:55, 3:46
ptarmigan, *2:82*
pteranodon, 3:80–81
public health, 2:56–57
puffer fish, *3:97*
pulley, 9:65, 9:88–89, 9:117

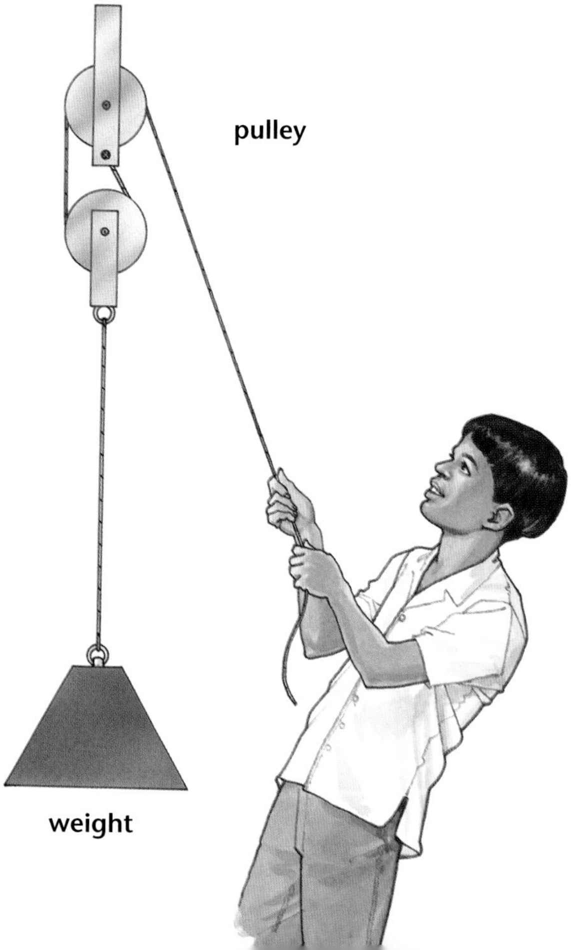

pulling, 9:68
pulsar, 7:29
pulse
electric, 8:17, 8:26, 8:29
human, 2:21
puma, *1:44*
pump, bicycle, 5:87
pumping station, *9:91*
punch press, *9:113*
pupa, 3:28, 3:34
pupil, of eye, *2:34*
puppet theater, 10:25
purple queen, *3:64*
pushing, 9:68, 9:70
puzzle, 7:82
pylon, 9:39
pyramid, 9:28–29
Pyrenees Mountains, *6:108*

Q

quartz, *5:22*

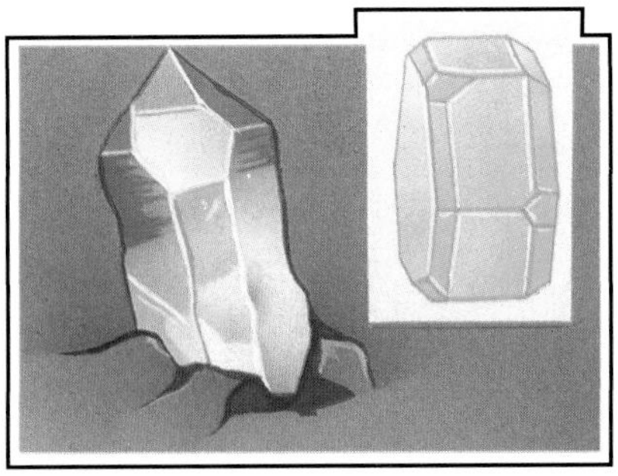

quartz

quasar, *7:29*
Queen Alexandra's birdwing butterfly, 2:75
queen bee, 3:27
Queen conch, *3:60*
queen termite, 3:26
questions, in calculating, *7:74–77*
quill, *3:97*
quillwort, *1:64*
quinine, 1:114

R

rabbit, *1:17, 1:30,* 4:46
race car driver, *9:14*
radiant energy, 4:20
radiant heat, 6:89
radiation
elecromagnetic, 4:114–117
heat, 2:86, 6:89, 8:95
radioactive, see **radioactivity**
radiation therapy, *5:61*
radiator, 6:89
radio, *4:79,* 8:34–41
broadcasting, 8:35–37
for astronaut, 7:52–53
on satellite, 7:39, 7:40
signals, 8:34
transistor, 8:42–43
tuning, 8:38–41
two-way, 8:53
radioactivity, 2:104–106, 5:60–61, 8:103
radiocarbon dating, 5:61
radio interferometry, 7:28
radio mast, 9:39
radio receiver, see **receiver**
radio relay station, 8:27
radio scanner, 8:39
radio signal, see **signal**
radio station, *4:117,* 8:36
radio telescope, 7:28
radio transmitter, 8:26, 8:34–36, 8:53
radio wave, *4:115,* 4:116–117, 8:34–37, 8:40–41, *8:48,* 8:80–81
rafflesia, *1:74*
raft, energy from, 8:110
raft foundation, *9:32*
railroad, see **train**
railroad tunnel, 9:46
railway bridge, *9:9*
rain, *6:38,* 6:43–45
acid, 2:98–99
rainbow, 4:14–15, *4:16*
rain forest, tropical, see **tropical rain forest**
RAM, see random access memory
ramp, 9:28

random access memory, *7:96–97*
rattlesnake, 4:22
ray (fish), 3:66
reaction, see **action and reaction**
reaction time, 2:42
reaction turbine, 8:104–105
reactor, 8:103
read-only memory, *7:96–97*
reasoning, 7:74
receiver, *8:34–35,* 8:36, 8:48, 8:58
receptacle, 1:94–95
receptor, in nose, 2:31
rechargeable battery, 4:55, 8:91, 8:93
reckoning, 7:74
record, database, 7:106
recordkeeping, 10:23, 10:26–27
rectifier, *4:105*
recycling, 2:110–117, *2:116,* 4:94
glass, 2:112
metal, 2:112, 4:94
paper, 2:112–113
plastic, 2:111

recycling waste

red (color), 4:16–17, 4:25, *4:39, 4:115, 8:46–47, 8:49*
red blood cell, 2:18, *2:51*
red coral, *3:8*
red fox, *3:89*
red giant (star), 7:16
red kangaroo, *3:90*
red panda, *3:90*
Red Planet, 7:22
Red Sea, *3:54*
Redwood National Park, 1:8–9, 1:73
reef, see **coral reef**
reentry, by spacecraft, 7:45
reference material, 10:12
refinery, 5:54–55, 5:112–113
reflecting telescope, 4:31, 7:26–27
reflection, 4:12–13, 4:18–19, 4:28–29
reflexes, 2:41
refracting telescope, 4:30, 7:26
refraction, 4:14–15, 4:26–27, 4:32, 4:39

refraction

refrigerator, 2:85
reinforced concrete, 9:23, 9:47
reinforcement, 9:24
relaxation, 2:61
relay, 8:12, 8:13
radio, 8:27
relay satellite, 8:13
remote control, *4:117*
renewable resource, 6:60–61
renewable source of energy, 8:67, 8:92
reproduction, 1:52–53
asexual, 1:52
as sign of life, 1:11
bird, 3:73
human, 2:46
invertebrate, 3:28, 3:48–49
plant, 1:94–107
sexual, 1:53
see also **life cycle**
reptile, 3:65, 3:70–71
ocean, 3:111

moloch (reptile)

Reptilia, *3:65*
repulsion, see **attraction and repulsion**
research scientist, 10:21
reservoir, 6:75, 9:50
resistance, 4:64, 4:112–113
resources, see **natural resources**
respiration, see **breathing**
retina, *2:26,* 2:34–35
revolution, of Earth, 6:36
rhinoceros, 2:75, *3:107*

great Indian rhinoceros

rhizoid, 1:90
rhombohedral crystal, *5:22*
rib bone, 2:12
ribbon worm, *3:8,* 3:14
rice, 1:112, *6:77,* 8:74
Richter scale, 6:21
ring
  around planet, 7:23
  on fish scale, 3:67
ringed plover, *3:96*
ringed seal, *2:82*
Rio Tinto, *2:101*
ripple, 6:98
river, 6:30, 6:31
  pollution of, 2:100–101, *2:116*
river animals, 3:112
road, 9:52–53
  as inclined plane, 9:78
road junction, 9:52
robot, 7:58, 7:114–115, 9:85, 9:114–117
rock, 1:58–59, *5:8,* 6:13
  erosion, 6:30–31
  formation of, 6:24–25
  in mountain formation, 6:18
  porous versus nonporous, 6:72–73
rocket, 5:82–83, 5:101, 7:32–35, 9:44
rocket booster, 7:46–47
Rock of Gibraltar, *10:14*
rodent, 3:88
rods, in eye, 2:35
roller coaster, *8:82*
rolling, of steel, 9:27
ROM, see **read-only memory**
Roman architecture, 9:35
root, 1:88–89, 1:104–105, 1:110, 6:93–94
root hair, 6:94
rope, 9:16
  measurement with, *10:37*
  with pulley, 9:88
rose, *1:12*
Ross seal, *2:83*
rosy periwinkle, 2:59
rotary pump, 9:100
rotary telephone, 8:26
rotating coil, *4:104*
rotation, of Earth, 6:36, 7:10
rotor, 8:101, 9:100
rotor blade, *9:94*
round-leaved crow plant, *1:67*
roundworm, *3:8,* 3:14
Rozier, Jean de, 5:74
rubber, 4:59, 5:58–59, 6:95
rubber band, *8:77*
rubber tree, 6:95
ruby, 6:56
rudder, 9:104
ruff, 3:95
ruler, *10:37*
runner (plant stem), 1:106
running, *5:92*
runway, *9:104–105*
rust, 5:40, 5:49, 5:60, 5:69, 6:110–111, 9:26

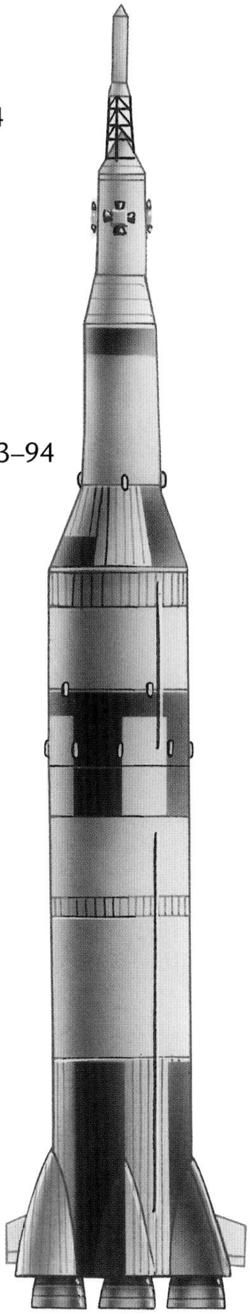

Saturn V rocket

S

sac, 1:42
saddle, bicycle, *9:86*
safety, in science activities, 10:28, 10:38–39

safety glasses, *10:9*
safety symbol, *10:39*
Sahara desert, 2:94–95
Sahel, 2:94
salad, 1:89
salamander, *3:97*
saliva, 1:38, *2:23*
salmon, 3:67
salt, *5:16,* 5:22, 6:104–105
taste of, 2:30
see also **salt water**
Salter, Stephen, 8:110
Salter duck, 8:110
salt pan, 6:48–49, *6:105*
salt water, 5:18–21
electricity and, 5:46–47
floating on, 6:104–105
life in, 1:68–69, 3:34, 3:46–55, 3:110–111, 6:48–50
saltwater fish, 3:67, 3:110
Salyut (space station), 7:54
sand dollar, 3:18
sandgrouse, *3:101*
sandstone, *9:18*
sanitary landfill, 5:111–112
sap, 1:47, 6:95
sapphire, 6:56
sarcodine, *1:13*
Sargasso Sea, 1:25, *3:94*
sargassum, 1:25
satellite (moon), 7:20
satellite, artificial, *6:15,* 7:37–43
Earth-survey, 7:38, 7:42
weather, 7:38
see also **communications satellite**
satellite dish, 8:59
saturated solution, 6:105
Saturn, 7:20–23, *7:60, 10:15*
Saturn V rocket, 7:34, 7:56
savanna, 1:78
saw, *9:112*
saxifrage, *2:82*
scaffold, *9:9*
scale (device), *7:72,* 10:36
scale (fish), 3:66

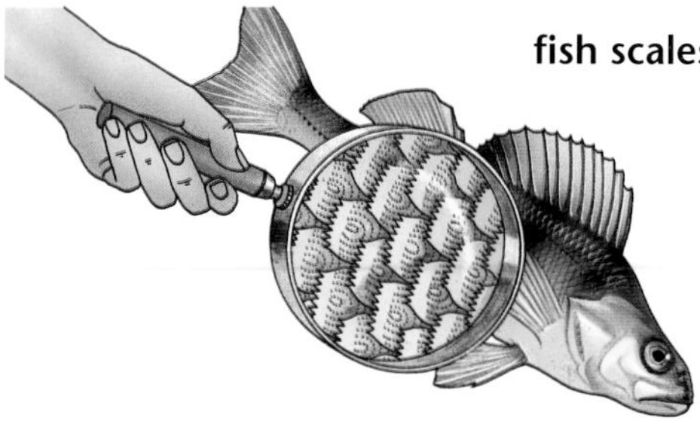

scale (layer), 6:108, 6:109
scanner, 4:41, *7:94,* 8:23
scanning, by television camera, 8:46, 8:48
SCARAB, 8:33
scarlet fever, *1:26*
scarlet macaw, *3:73*
scavenger, 3:19, 3:43
schistosomiasis, *2:55,* 3:15
science
areas of, 10:20–21
definition of, 10:12–13
things studied by, 10:14–19
see also **scientist**
scientist, 10:9
becoming, 10:23
equipment for, 10:24–25, 10:28–29, 10:36–37
in team, 10:21
materials for, 10:30–31
measurement by, 10:32–37
recordkeeping by, 10:23, 10:26–27
safety for, 10:38–39
work area for, 10:24–25
scorpion, 3:22, 3:36, *3:45*
scrapyard, 4:94
scratch, on skin, *2:57*
screw, 9:65, 9:80–81

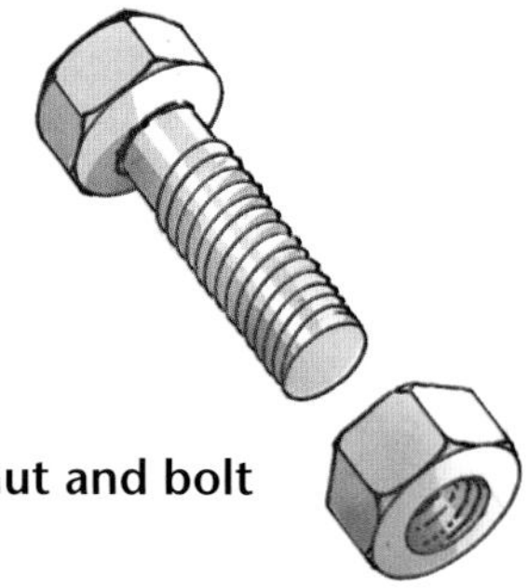

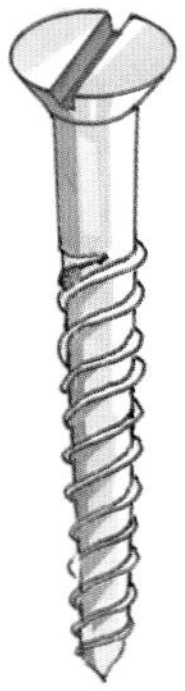

shoot

silicon, *5:13*
silicon chip, see **chip, electronic**
silver, 4:59, 6:52, 6:55
silver salts, 6:50
simple eye, 4:47
simple machines, 9:65
  energy for, 9:90–92
  inclined plane, 9:78–79
  lever, 9:67, 9:72–77
  pulley, 9:87–89
  screw, 9:80–81
  wedge, 9:79
  wheel and axle, 9:82–87
simulator, 7:51, *7:112*
siphon, 6:69
skate, 3:110
skater, *8:76*
skeleton, 3:78–79
  human, 2:12, *3:79*
skin, human, *2:26,* 2:27, 2:32–33
  melanin in, 4:21
skin cancer, 2:84
skin cell, *1:21*
skua, Arctic, *2:82*
sky, 7:9
  color of, 4:38–39
Skylab, 7:54
skyscraper, 9:42–43
sky wave, 8:35
slag, 5:45
sleep, 2:61, 3:90–91
sleeping sickness, 2:54
slip ring, 4:106–107
slope, 9:78
sloth, 3:108
slow combustion, 5:94
slow-growing plant, 1:81
sludge, *6:82*
sludge tank, *6:83*
slug, 3:20
small intestine, 1:38–39, 2:19, *2:23*
smell, *2:26,* 2:31
smelting, 5:44–45, *6:54*
smog, 2:96

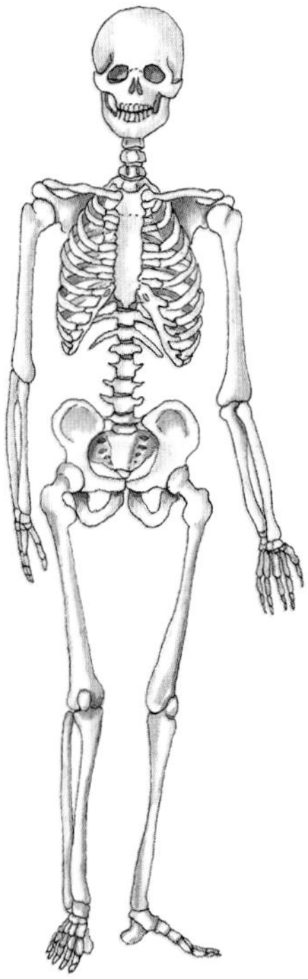

human skeleton

smooth muscle, 2:15
smooth newt, *3:64*
snail, *1:12, 1:46,* 3:20–21, 3:37, 3:46–47
  land, *3:9, 3:61*
  shell of, *9:8*
snake, *1:14, 1:17, 3:65,* 3:70, 3:97, *3:101,* 3:111
sneezing, *2:49, 2:57*
snowflake, *6:84,* 6:90
snow leopard, 3:105, *3:117*
snow petrel, *2:83*
snowy owl, *2:82*
soccer, 7:80
socket, electric, 4:58
soda ash, 6:109
sodium, *5:13, 5:16–17,* 5:19, 5:20, 6:54
sodium bicarbonate, see **bicarbonate of soda**
sodium carbonate, 5:43, 6:109
sodium chloride, 5:20, 6:104
  see also **salt**
sodium hydroxide, 5:24, 5:47
sodium hypochlorite, 5:47
software, 7:84, 7:98–102, 8:61
soil, 1:32–35, 6:92
  building construction and, 9:32, 9:52
  composition of, 1:86–87
  nutrients, 2:88
  overgrazing, 2:89, 2:94, 2:95, *2:116*
  plant needs, 1:82–83, 1:87
  porous versus nonporous, 6:72–73
  protecting, 2:93
  rain forest, 2:79
  testing, 2:92

soil sample

solar battery, 8:50
solar cell, 8:85, *8:107*
solar cell panel, 7:39
solar energy, 2:98, 4:74–75, 8:67, 8:85, 8:92, 8:106–107

satellite powered by, 8:50
solar furnace, 8:107
solar panel, 8:50, 8:67, *8:85*
solar power, see **solar energy**
solar-powered calculator, *4:116*
solar storm, 7:11
solar system, 6:10, 7:20–21
origins, 6:10–11
solder, *5:16*
soldering, 6:55
soldier termite, 3:26–27
solenoid, 4:98–101
solid, 5:26–27, 5:65, 6:84, 6:90
melting and freezing, 5:28–29
soluble substance, 5:18, 6:105

solute, 5:18
solution, 5:18–19, 6:80, 6:94, 6:104
solvent, 5:18
sore throat, *1:26*
SOS, 8:17
sound, 8:78–79
speed of, 6:45
wave of, 8:10–11, 8:24, 8:25, 8:78
sounder, on telegraph, 8:20
sour taste, 2:30
South African cycad, *1:93*
Southern Cross, 4:90, 7:14
Southern Hemisphere, *6:36–37*
south magnetic pole (Earth), 4:86
South Pole (Earth), 4:86, 6:32, 6:36–37, *6:90*
south pole, of magnet, 4:81, 4:82, 4:96
space, 5:9, 10:15
definition of, 7:9
gases in, 5:108–109
laws of, 7:30–31
measurement, 7:31
studying, 7:9
working in, 7:52–53
see also **space travel**
spacecraft, 7:44
computer and, 7:105, 7:113
lunar, 7:56–57
reentry by, 7:45
see also **space travel** and specific spacecraft
Spacelab, 7:54
space probe, 7:58–61, 7:115
space shuttle, *6:15*, 7:45, 7:48, 7:54
training for, 7:50–51

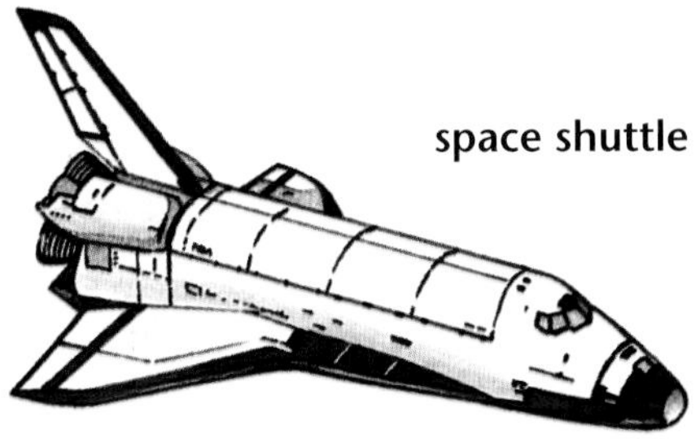

space sickness, 7:49
space station, 7:54–55
spacesuit, 7:52–53
space telescope, 7:29
space trash, 8:51
space travel, 7:44–61
effects of, 7:48–49
to moon, 7:56–57
training for, 7:50–51
see also **spacecraft**
spacewalk, 7:52
Spaghetti Junction (United Kingdom), *9:52*
span, 9:8
span bridge, 9:34
spawn, 3:68
speaker
answering machine, *8:54*
radio, 8:41
species, 1:16, 2:72, 3:66

spectrum, 4:16
electromagnetic, 4:20, 4:116–117
invisible, 4:20
visible, 4:20

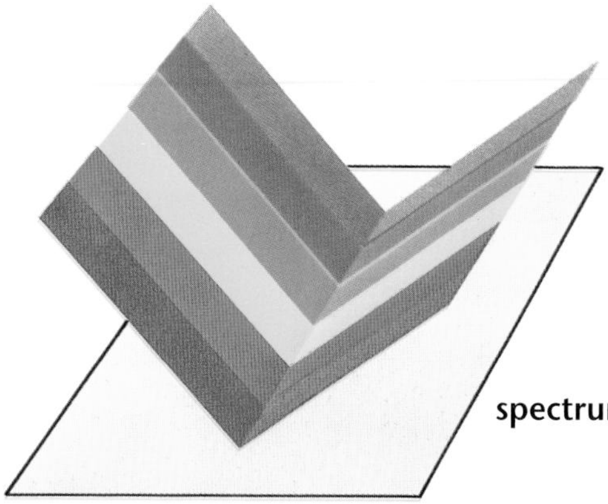

spectrum

speed
of light, 4:36–37, 6:45, 7:31, 8:51, 8:81
of sound, 6:45
sperm, 1:53, 1:94, 3:36
sphere, 9:10–11
spider, *1:12, 1:15, 1:43, 3:9,* 3:22, 3:36
digestion by, 1:39
tarantula, *3:45*

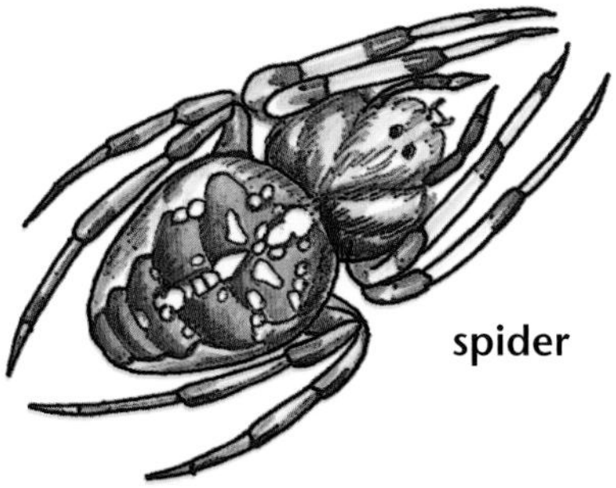

spider

spider monkey, 3:108
spider web, *1:15*
spinal column, 3:64, 3:66, 3:76–77
spinal cord, 2:40, 2:41, 3:76
spine, see **spinal column**
spineless cactus, *10:9*
spiny-tailed lizard, *3:101*
spiral, 9:25
spiral galaxy, 7:19
spiral staircase, 9:25
spirella, *1:13*
spirogyra, 1:24
splitting, 1:52
sponge, *3:8,* 3:10–11, 3:46, 3:48–49
spool tractor, 8:77
spoon, as lever, 9:72
sporangia, *1:91*
spore, 1:90–91, 1:107
SPOT (satellite), 7:42
spring (device), 8:91, *9:85*
spring (season), 6:36–37
spring (water), *8:112*
spring balance, *10:36*
spring-driven clock, 9:85
springtail, 1:35, *3:25*
spring tide, 6:29
spring water, *6:80–81*
sprinkler, 6:115
sprocket, bicycle, *9:86*
spruce, *1:93, 1:96*
Sputnik 1, 7:38
square centimeter, 10:34
square foot, 10:34
squid, *3:9,* 3:20, 3:46–47
squirrel, *1:30,* 8:90
squirt power, 6:114–115
staghorn coral, *1:12*
stainless steel, *9:26*
stalk, *1:94*
stamen, *1:94*
star, 5:109, 7:14–19
distance to, 7:31
energy from, 8:94
life of, 7:16–17
sizes, 7:15
sun as, 7:11
See also **constellation; galaxy**
starch, 1:84, 1:112
star cluster, 7:15
starfish, 1:37, *3:9,* 3:18, 3:46–47, 3:51

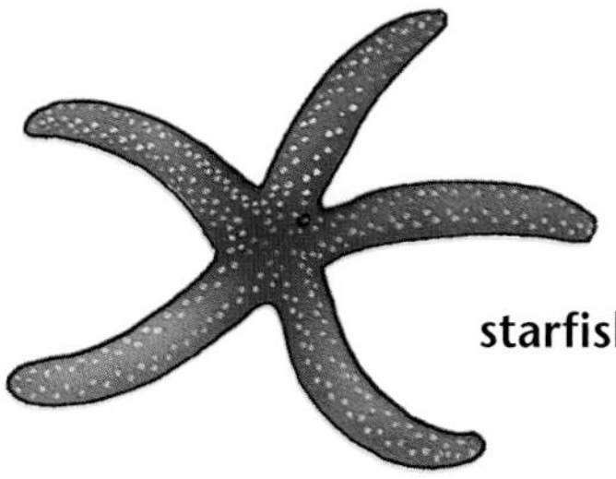

starfish

star viewer, 7:15
stator, 8:101
stator blade, *9:94*
Statue of Liberty, *9:26–27*
steak, *6:79*
steam, 5:30, 6:84, 6:88, 6:89, 8:69, *9:57*
energy from, 4:75, 6:117, 8:100, 8:112–113
geyser, 6:23
steamboat, *9:91*
steam engine, 8:69, 8:91, 9:90–93, 10:17
steam turbine, 9:94
steel, 5:44–45, 6:54, 6:103, *8:68*, 9:12, 9:19
as reinforcement, 9:23, 9:24, 9:47
frame of, 9:26–27, 9:42
in oil platform, 9:40
in skyscraper, 9:42
steering, 9:87, 9:98
stem, 1:88–89
stem rust, *1:55*
step, in reasoning, 7:76–79, 7:100
step-down transformer, 4:72
steppe, 1:78
step-up transformer, 4:72
stereo, *7:86*
stereoscopic vision, 2:37, 4:46
stigma, 1:94–95, 1:99
stimulated emission, 4:40
stinging thread, *3:12*
stirrup, of ear, 2:28–29
stock prices, 8:22
stoma, *1:43*

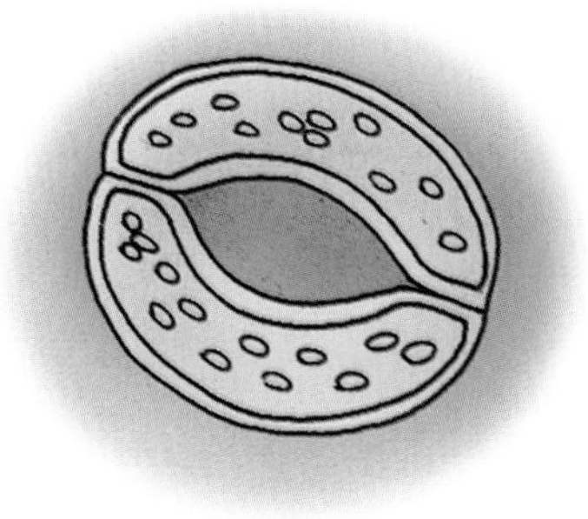

leaf stoma

stomach, 1:38–39, *2:22–23*
stomata, 1:43, 1:66, 1:84, 1:88
stone, as building material, 9:18
Stonehenge, *9:29*
storage battery, 8:91
storm, 6:44–45, 6:99
strangler fig, 1:81
stratopause, 6:14–15
stratosphere, 5:70–71, 6:14–15
strawberry plant, 1:106
streamlined shape, 6:100, 7:38
street lamp, 9:44
string
measurement with, *10:37*
piano, 9:76
striped muscle, 2:15
striped pyxie toad, *3:101*
stroke, of piston, 9:96
structural engineer, 9:26, 9:30
structure, 9:8–61
containing, 9:14–15
definition of, 9:8–9
early, 9:18, 9:28–29
forces on, 9:16–17, 9:22–23, 9:42
foundation for, 9:32–33
future, 9:60–61
insulating, 9:58–59
materials in, see **materials, construction**
planning, 9:30–31
reinforcing, 9:24–25
shapes in, 9:10–11
underground, 9:54–55
waterproofing, 9:56–57
sturgeon, *3:117*
style, 1:94–95
subgrade, 9:53
submarine, 4:29, 6:101
substance, 5:9
succulent plant, 1:71
sucker, 3:18–19, 3:21
Sudan, *6:77*
sugar, 1:45, 5:34
sugar cane, 1:112, 8:115
sulfur, 5:42, 5:58–59
sulfur dioxide, 2:96, 2:97
sulfuric acid, 2:98, 5:24, 5:42
summer, 6:36–37
sun, 5:109, 7:11, *7:60*
as energy source, 8:64, 8:71, 8:94–95, 8:97
as light source, 4:8, 4:14
burning out, 8:95

sun (continued)
climate and, 6:42, 6:43
energy and, 2:98, 6:9, 6:43, 6:66
exploration of, 7:58
gravitational force of, 7:30
heliograph message using, 8:18
importance of, 7:10
magnetism and, *4:85,* 4:87
nuclear fusion in, 8:73, 8:95
nuclear reactions on, 6:11
origins of, 6:10
seasons and, 6:36–37
sky color and rays from, 4:38–39
structure of, 8:95
tide and, 6:29
ultraviolet rays of, 2:84
see also **solar energy; sunlight**

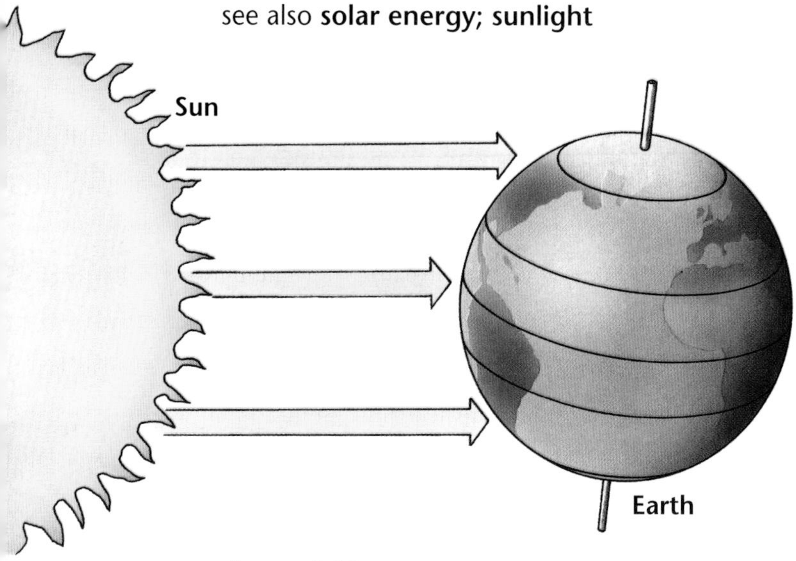

sunburn, 4:21
sundew plant, *1:11*
sunfish, *3:64*
sunflower, 4:18, 5:9
sunlight
food production and, 1:12
plants and, 1:84
sunrise, 4:39
sunset, 4:38–39
sunspot, 7:11
sun star, *3:9*
supercomputer, 7:90
superconductor, 4:112–113
superfluid, 5:101
supergiant, 7:15
supernova, 7:16
support, by structure, 9:8
surface tension, 6:96–97
surgery, 4:41
survival, 1:60
suspension
automobile, 9:98–99
bicycle, 9:86
suspension bridge, 9:36–37
swallow, *3:72,* 3:95
swallowtail butterfly, *3:9*
swamp, 1:67–69, *1:116*
swamp plant, 1:67
swan, *1:10*
sweat gland, 2:33
sweating, 2:33, 3:99
sweep net, 3:38
sweet taste, 2:30
swift, *3:72, 3:83,* 3:95, 3:105
swimming, 6:102
by fish, 3:84–85
swimming crab, *3:9*
switch, electric, 4:66, 4:100, 8:17, 8:27, 8:29
synovial fluid, 2:13
syntax, 7:100
synthetic material, 5:56

T

tadpole, 3:69
tail, of comet, 7:25
Taj Mahal, *4:28,* 9:48
tallying, 7:66–67
tamandua, *3:109*
tamarin, lion, 2:72–73
tanker, *5:53, 8:93*
tape measure, *7:72*
tapeworm, *2:55,* 3:15
tarantula, *3:45*
taste, *2:26,* 2:30
taste bud, *2:26,* 2:30
Taurus (constellation), 7:14–15

tea, *1:111*
technology, 10:11, 10:16–17
tectonic plate, 6:17, 6:20, 6:23
telecommunication, 8:9, 8:60
see also specific types

telecommunications satellite dish

telegram, 8:20
telegraph, 8:9, 8:12, 8:16–17, 8:20–23
Telegraph Hill, *8:15*
telephone, 4:45, *7:87*, 8:8–9, 8:24–31
cellular, 8:52
cordless, 8:53
dialing, 8:26
extension, 8:30
parts of, 8:25
sharing lines, 8:28
string, 8:30–31
touch-tone, 8:26, 8:58
see also **videophone**
telephone cable, 9:54
telephone exchange, 8:26–29
telephone number, 8:26
telephone pole, *4:50*
telephoto, 8:23
teleprinter, 8:23
telescope, 4:30–31, 7:26–29
teletypewriter, 8:23
television, 4:22, *7:86–87*, 7:110, 8:9, 8:46–49, 8:58
cable, 8:59
high-definition, 8:59
satellite dish, 8:59
television station, *4:117*
television studio, *8:47*
television tube, 8:48
Telex, 8:23
temperature, 7:72
air pressure and, 5:80
altitude and, 5:71
body, 2:27
boiling point, 6:88
feeling, 2:32
freezing point, 6:90
kindling, 5:94
on Earth, 6:38, 7:11, 7:42
on sun, 7:11
temperature changes
form of matter and, 5:26–32
gases and, 5:26–27, 5:30–34, 5:84–85, 5:100–101
temple, 9:28–29
tensile strength, 9:16
tension, 9:16–17, 9:22–23
tent, *9:9*
tentacle, 3:12, *3:13*
Teotihuacán, *9:29*
terminal, battery, 4:53
terminal, computer, 7:90
termite, 1:37, 3:26–27
tern, *3:73, 3:94*
Terra (satellite), 7:42
terrestrial planet, 7:23
test (shell), 3:19
tetragonal crystal, *5:22*
TGV train, *4:105*
theory, 10:13
thermic lance, 5:105
thermogram, 4:23
thermometer, *7:72*
thermosphere, 5:71, 6:14–15
thorax, of insect, 3:24–25
thread, on screw, 9:80
throttle, 9:104
thrust, 5:82–83

thunder, 6:45
thundercloud, 6:44, 6:46
thunderstorm, 6:44–45
thyroid gland, *2:45*
tidal power station, 8:110–111
tide, 6:28–29, 8:110–111
tide pool, 3:53
tie-rod, 9:98
tiger, 1:12, *1:14*, 1:16, 2:74, *3:96*
tiger lily, *1:65*
time, 7:72, 9:67, 10:32–33, 10:36
tin, *5:17*, 6:55, *6:61*
tire, bicycle, *9:86*
tissue, human, 2:11
tit, *1:12*
Titan, 7:61
titanium, 6:54
toad, *3:101*
Tokyo, 9:42
tomato, *1:110*, *6:79*, 8:74
ton, 10:33
toner, printer, 7:103
tongue, *2:26*, 2:30
tongue fern, *1:12*
tool, 9:13, *9:83*
tooth, 3:88–89
topaz, *5:22*

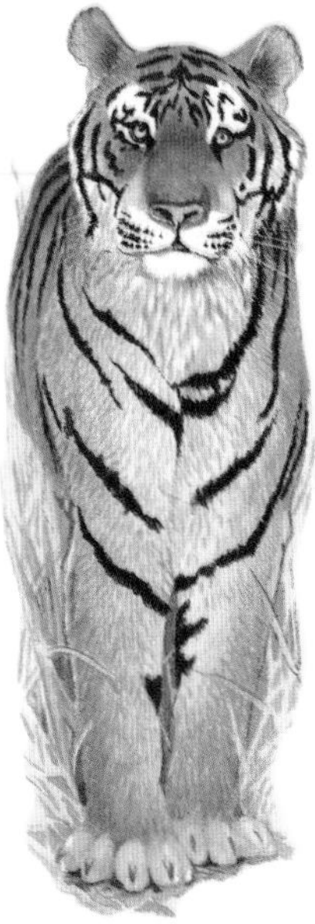

tiger

topaz

topsoil, 2:93
tornado, *5:73*, 6:46
tortoise, 3:71
toucan, *3:65*, *3:108*, *3:109*
touch, *2:26*, 2:32
touch screen, *7:95*
touch-tone telephone, 8:26, 8:58
tower, 9:44–45
toy, clockwork, 9:85
trace element, 6:80
trachea, 2:16–17
trackball, *7:95*
Tracking and Data Relay Satellite, 7:41
tracking satellite, 7:40
tractor, *8:116*, 9:82
Trafalgar, Battle of, 8:15
traffic light, *7:74–75*
train, *4:79*, *4:105*, 4:110–111, 8:69
transatlantic cable, *8:32*
transformer, 4:72–73
transistor, 8:42–43
translucent plastic, 4:19
transmission
  automobile, 9:98–99
  bicycle, 9:86
  satellite, 7:39
transmitter
  radio, 8:26, 8:34–36, 9:39
  satellite, 8:26, 8:48
  television, *8:47*, 8:48
transpiration, 1:88, 6:66–67
transportation, 2:97, *2:117*
  water, 6:117
treated water, 6:82
tree, 1:77, 6:60, 6:61, *9:8*
  deciduous, 1:73
  evergreen, 1:72
  largest, 1:9, 1:73
  see also specific trees
tree buttress, 9:25
tree fern, *1:64*, *1:91*
tree frog, 3:109
trench, *6:27*, 9:28
triangle, in construction, 9:39
triceps, 1:48, 2:15
trichinosis, *2:55*
triclinic crystal, *5:22*
trilobite, *1:59*
tropical climate, *6:43*
tropical rain forest, 1:74–75, 2:78–81, *9:61*
  destruction of, *2:73*, 2:79
  invertebrates in, 3:42–43
  medicine from, 2:59

saving, 2:80–81
vertebrates in, 3:108–109
Tropic of Cancer, 6:42
Tropic of Capricorn, 6:42
tropopause, 6:14–15
troposphere, 5:70, 6:14–15
trunk, tree, 1:77
tsetse fly, 2:54
tsunami, 6:21
tuatara, 3:71
tube foot, 3:18
tuber, 1:106
tuberculosis, 1:55
tube sponge, *3:8*
tubeworm, 3:59
tundra, 1:70
tuner, 8:38–39, *8:48*
tungsten, 4:64, 5:116, 9:113
Tunisia, *4:27*
tunnel, *9:9*, 9:46–47
tunneling machine, 9:46, 9:47
tunnel network, 9:54
turbine, 4:70–71, 8:69, *8:92*, 8:100, 8:104–105, 9:94–95

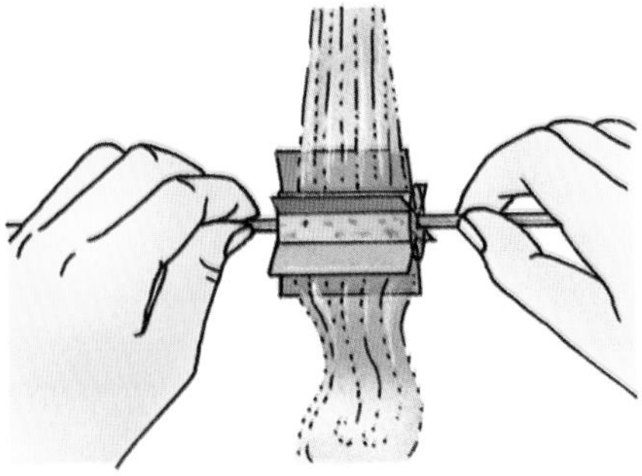

water turbine

turbulence, 6:100–101
turtle, *3:65*, 3:71, 3:111, *3:116*
TV, see **television**
twister, see **tornado**
two-way radio, 8:53
type (printing), 9:110
typhoon, 6:47
Tyrannosaurus rex, *3:80*

U

UHF radio wave, 8:35
ultraviolet rays, 2:84, 4:20–21, 4:47, 4:116–117
ultraviolet telescope, *7:29*
ultraviolet wave, *8:80*
Ulysses (space probe), 7:58
umbilical cord, 2:46–47
underground structures, 9:54–55
underground water, 6:72–73
see also **groundwater**
undersea cable, 8:32–33
uniform resource locator, 7:109
unit, 7:68
of measurement, 7:72, 7:73, 10:32–34
United Kingdom, *6:81*
and Channel Tunnel, 9:46
universe, expanding, 7:18
uranium, 8:73, *8:102–103*
Uranus, 7:20–23, **7:61**
urban spread, 2:67
urea, 2:24
ureter, 2:19, 2:24–25
urethra, 2:19, 2:24–25
urine, 1:40, 2:19, 2:24–25
URL, 7:109
Ursa Major, 7:14
Ursa Minor, 7:14
Utah, *6:31*
uterus, 2:46–47

V

V-2 guided missile, *7:35*
vaccination, 2:52
vagina, 2:47
valley glacier, 6:34–35
valve, 2:18, *2:20*, 5:87
valve box, 9:54–55
vane (gas pump), 9:100
vapor, 5:84
see also **water vapor**
vascular plant, 1:88

vascular system, 1:88
vascular tissue, 1:88
VCR, 4:22, 7:86–87
vegetarian, 1:11

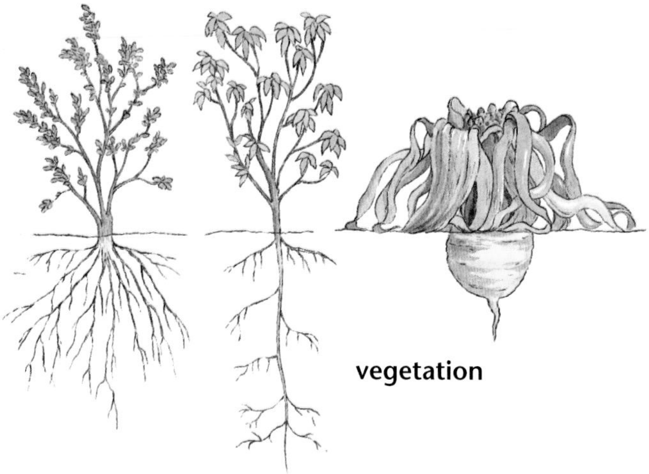

vegetation

vegetative propagation, 1:106
vein, 2:18

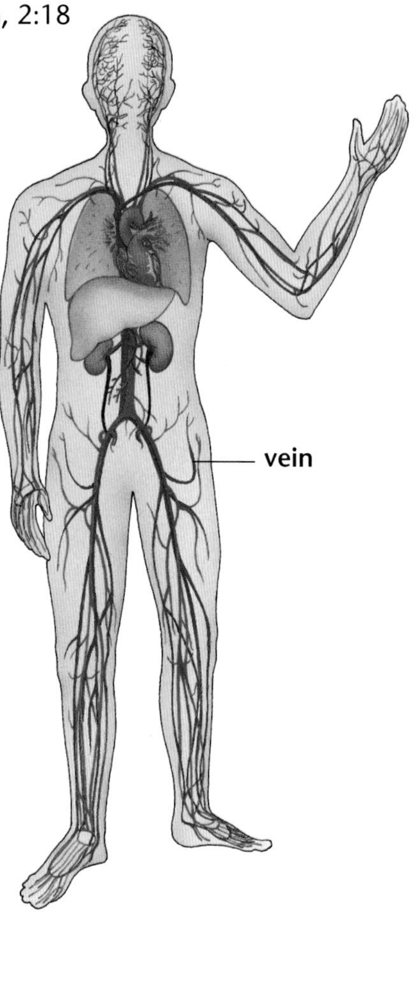

vein

velocity, 7:36
velvet worm, *3:42*
Venera (space probe), 7:59
ventilation, 9:46, 9:58
Venus, 7:20–23, 7:58, 7:59
Venus's-flytrap, 1:81
verge, on pendulum clock, *9:84*
Verrazano Narrows suspension bridge, *9:36*
vertebrae, 3:76
vertebrate, 3:63–117
by place
forests, 3:108–109
grasslands, 3:106–107
islands, 3:114–115
lakes and rivers, 3:112–113
mountains, 3:104–105
oceans, 3:110–111
polar regions, 3:102–103
defenses of, 3:96–97
definition of, 3:8, 3:64–65
keeping warm or cool, 3:98–99
need for oxygen, 3:86–87
prehistoric, 3:80–81
senses of, 3:92–93
sleeping by, 3:90–91
travel by, 3:94–95
see also specific types

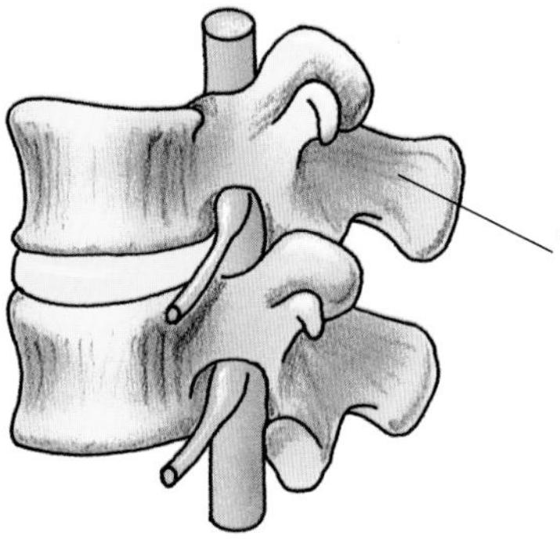

vertebra

Very Large Telescope, 7:27–28
vestibule, of ear, 2:28, 2:29
VHF radio wave, 8:35
vibration
of atoms, and heat, 8:88
of piano string, *9:76*
sound, 8:10–11, 8:41, 8:79

videocassette recorder, 4:22, 7:86–87
video game, *7:87*
video game controller, *8:44*
videophone, 8:58
Vietnam forests, 2:81
viewfinder, camera, 4:34
Viking (space probes), 7:59
vine, 1:77
vinegar, 5:38–39, 5:41, 5:48
vinegar eel, 3:14
violet, 4:16, 4:25, *4:39*
virtual reality, 7:110–111
virus, 1:19, 2:48–49, 2:52
virus, computer, 7:99
vision, 2:34–37, 4:46–47
  see also **eye; sight**
visual BASIC, 7:100
vitamin, 2:22
vitamin D, 4:9, 4:21
VLT, *7:27–28*
voice coil, 8:41
voice mail, 8:55
voice messaging system, 8:55
voice recognition system, *7:94*
volcanic island, *6:27*
volcano, 4:38, 6:20, 6:22–23
  in ocean, *6:27*
Volta, Alessandro, 4:60
volt and voltage, 4:60–61, 4:72
volume, 6:90, 6:102, 7:72, 10:35
voluntary muscle, 2:15
volvox, 1:24
Vostok 1, 7:44
Voyager (space probe), 7:60–61
vulcanization, 5:59
vulture, *3:65*

W

wakame, *1:25*
walking catfish, 3:67
wall, *9:9, 9:20, 9:33*
wallaby, *3:75*
walrus, *2:82*, 3:111
WAN, 7:107
waning moon, 7:13
warbler, *3:73*
warm-blooded animal, 3:98
warning color, 1:57
washing hands, *2:56*
wasp, 3:57
waste
  animal, 1:40–41, 1:101
  gases from, 5:111
  human body, 2:24–25
  industrial, 2:102, 2:103, 2:109
  nuclear, 2:105–107
  sources, 2:108–109
  see also **decay and decomposition; pollution; recycling**
watch, *7:86*, 8:107, *10:36*
water, 6:63–117
  amount on Earth's surface, 6:65
  as force for motion, 6:114–115
  boiling, 5:30, 6:88
  city supply of, 9:54
  conserving, *2:114–115*
  corrosion by, 6:110–111
  energy from, 2:98, 8:69, 8:85, 8:101, 8:104–105, 8:110–111, 9:50
  erosion by, 6:30–31
  evaporation of, see **evaporation**
  floating versus sinking in, 6:102–103, 6:106–107
  flow, 6:68–69, 6:116–117
  food production and, 1:12, 1:84
  hard versus soft, 6:108–109
  heating with, 6:89
  human body and, 2:11, 6:78–81
  in agriculture, 6:92–95
  in plant, 6:94–95
  level of, 6:68–71, 6:70
  life and, 1:11
  molecule of, *5:16*, 5:27, 6:84, 6:96, 6:97
  pollution of, see **water pollution**
  protecting buildings from, 9:56–57
  safety of, *2:57*, 6:74–75
  states of, 6:65, 6:84–85

water (continued)
storing, 6:75
surface of, 6:69
surface tension, 6:96–97
temperature changes in, 5:26–32
travel through, 6:100–101
underground, 6:23, 6:72–73
uses for, 6:76–77, 6:116–117
waste, 6:82–83
see also **fresh water; ice; liquid; ocean; salt water; water vapor**
waterbird, 3:113
water boatman, 3:34
water cycle, 6:66–67
water erosion, 2:93
waterfall, *6:68, 6:84*
water filter, 6:75

water filter

water lily, 1:66
water main, *9:54–55*
watermill, 6:116
water opossum, *3:112*
water plant, 1:66
water pollution, 2:100–103, *2:116,* 6:61, 6:82
waterproofing, 6:112–113
water scorpion, *3:34*
water spider, *1:43*
water strider, *6:96*
water treatment plant, 6:75
water turbine, 6:116
water vapor, 5:32, 5:84, 5:106–107, 6:65, 6:86, 6:90
energy from, 8:100, *8:112*
weather and, *6:38,* 6:43
waterwheel, 4:74, 6:116–117, 8:85, 8:104
wave
electromagnetic, 4:20, 4:114–117, 8:80–81
light, 4:12, 4:16, 8:46, 8:80–81
ocean, 6:28–29, 6:98–99, 8:110–111
radio, see **radio wave**

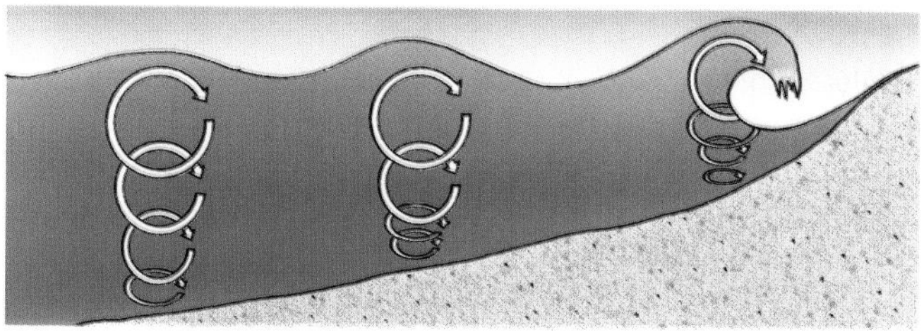

sea waves

waveband, 8:38–39
wavelength, 4:16, 4:115, 8:34, 8:37–38, 8:53
wax, *4:10*
waxing moon, 7:13
weather, 6:38–41
climate versus, 6:42
hurricane, 6:47
prediction of, 6:40–41
stormy, 6:44–45
tornado, 6:46
weather satellite, 7:38
Web, see **World Wide Web**
web (spider), 9:8
web browser, 7:109
web of life, 3:61
Web site, 7:108–109, 8:60

Weddell seal, *2:83*
wedge, 9:65, 9:78–79

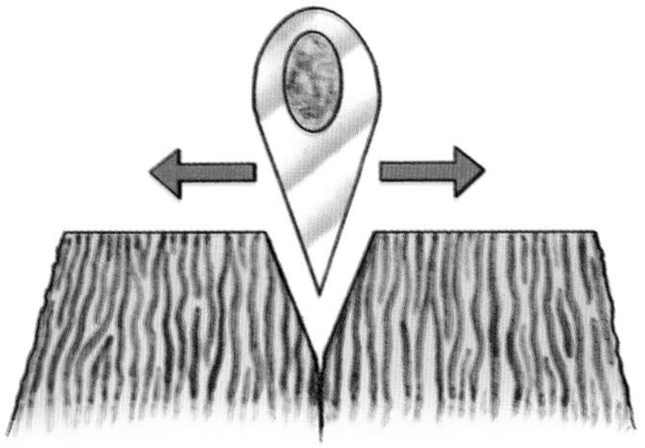

wedge

weedkiller, 2:90
weevil, *3:45,* 3:56
Wegener, Alfred, 6:16
weight, 7:72, 10:32
and floating, 6:103
weight, on pendulum clock, *9:84*
weight-driven clock, 9:84
weightlessness, 7:48–50, 7:54
welding, *4:63,* 5:96–97, 5:104–105
welwitschia, 6:93
welwitschia plant, 1:80
whale, *1:17, 3:74,* 3:90, 3:95
blue, 2:75, *2:83, 3:74*
bowhead, *2:82*
whale shark, *3:66*
whale skeleton, *3:78*
wheat, *1:65,* 1:112
wheel, 9:65, 9:82–87, 10:17
wheelbarrow, 9:72, 9:78
whippoorwill, *3:96*
white, 4:14–15, *4:17,* 4:18, *4:19,* 4:25
white blood cell, 1:56, 2:18, *2:51*
white dwarf, 7:16, 7:29
white-lipped peccary, *3:90*
wide area network, 7:107
wild cat, *1:17*
wildebeest, 3:95, *3:107*
wildflower, *2:76*
willow, *1:70*
winch, *9:82*
wind, 5:66, 5:72–73, 6:38–39, *6:87*
as force on buildings, 9:42, *9:44*
energy from, *2:117, 8:64,* 8:67, 8:92, 8:108–109
hurricane, 6:47
pollination by, 1:99, 1:100, *1:101*
wind farm, 8:109
wind generator, *2:117*
windlass, *9:82*
windmill, 4:74–75, 5:72, *8:64,* 8:108
window, 9:58
wind scorpion, 3:44
wind turbine, *8:92,* 8:108–109
winter, 6:36–37
wire, electrical, 4:58–59, 4:64, 4:112, 8:93, *8:99*
see also **cable**
wireless, 8:36
wolf, *1:17*
wolf spider, 3:36
wood, 5:94, 9:18, 10:30
energy from, 4:74, 8:67
woodcock, 2:36
woodland, 9:61
invertebrates in, 3:40–41
vertebrates in, 3:108–109
wood louse, 1:35, 3:22, 3:33, 3:37, 10:26
woodpecker, *3:117*
wood turtle, *3:71*
woody perennial, 1:109
woody plant, 1:77, 1:109
word-processing software, 7:102–103
work (physics), 8:86–87, 9:67, *9:79*
worker bee, 3:27
worker termite, 3:26
World Wide Web, 7:65, 7:100, 7:108–109, 8:60
see also **Internet**
worm, 2:48, 2:54–55, 3:8, 3:14–17, *3:42, 3:47, 3:53*
see also **earthworm; flatworm; tubeworm**
worm casting, 3:16, *3:53*
wormery, 3:17
wrench, *9:83*

X

xenon, 5:117
X-ray crystallographer, 10:21
X rays, 4:116–117, 8:80
X-ray telescope, *7:29*
xylem, 1:47

Y

yard, 10:33
yardstick, *10:37*
year, 6:36–37, 7:20
yeast, 1:112–113

yeast

yellow (color), *4:17,* 4:18, *4:19*
yellow dwarf (star), 7:15
yellow fever, *2:54–55*
Yellowstone National Park, *6:85*
"Yogi" (rock), *7:59*
yoke (wheel), 9:104–105

Z

zebra, *3:106*
ziggurat, 9:28
Zimbabwe, *6:116*
zinc, 6:52, *6:61*
zinc-carbon battery, 4:54
Zip disk, *7:99*
zircon, *5:22*

zircon

zone, earthquake, 6:20
zoologist, 10:20
zooplankton, 3:46–47

Glossary

Many important terms are used in *Young Scientist.* This glossary explains some of the more difficult ones.

A

acid is a *solid*, *liquid*, or *gas* that can dissolve in water. Vinegar and lemon juice are acidic *solutions*. All acids will turn an indicator dye the same color (opposite to *alkalis*). Some acids dissolve substances called bicarbonates, giving off carbon dioxide gas. All acids that are safe to taste are sour. When the right amount of an acid is mixed with an alkali, it becomes neutral. This means that the acid no longer has its acidic properties.

aerial means "in the air." 1. An aerial is a wire that receives or sends out radio waves. 2. Some plants have aerial roots that grow above the soil.

air pressure is the weight of all the air in the *atmosphere* pressing down on the surface of an object. Air pressure is greatest at sea level. High in the atmosphere, the pressure is low.

alkali is a *solid*, *liquid*, or *gas* that usually dissolves in water. Baking soda, soap, and detergent all make alkaline *solutions* when dissolved in water. All alkalis will turn an indicating solution the same color (opposite to acids). When the right amount of an alkali is mixed with an acid, it becomes neutral. This means that the alkali no longer has its alkaline properties.

alloy is a metal made by mixing different types of metal, or a metal with a nonmetal. Bronze is an alloy made by mixing tin and copper. An alloy has different properties from the materials that make up the alloy. Strong steel is made by mixing the metal iron with other metals and a nonmetal called carbon.

alternating current (AC) is an electric current that changes direction as it travels through a wire. AC supplied to homes in many countries changes direction 120 times every second.

ammeter is a special measuring device used to measure an *electric current.*

amp is short for *ampère*, It is a unit used to measure the size of an electric current. About half an amp flows through a small flashlight bulb. The current in overhead power lines is many hundreds of amps.

ampère is a unit for measuring the flow of an *electric current.*

analogue means similar or like. An analogue instrument is a model of the original. A watch with a dial and hands tells us the time. It is an analogue model of Earth. The movement of the hour hand matches the movement of Earth as it turns on its *axis.* The opposite of analogue is *digital.*

antenna is a long, thin device for picking up signals. 1. An insect has a pair of antennae on its head. 2. A radio has an antenna, or *aerial*, to pick up signals from radio stations.

antibody is a substance that our blood produces to defend our bodies against *microbes.*

atmosphere is a layer of *gases* surrounding an object. The gases inside an object can also be called its atmosphere. 1. The atmosphere around Earth is made up of the troposphere near Earth's surface, the stratosphere, the mesosphere, and the thermosphere. The four main gases that make up Earth's atmosphere are nitrogen, oxygen, carbon dioxide, and argon. 2. In space, there is no atmosphere.

B

bacteria are tiny living things. Each bacterium is made from a single *cell* that is so small, you can only see it under a microscope.

basalt is a rock that forms when molten rock from underground rises to the surface and cools.

binary means made up of two parts. A binary code is a system that uses only two numbers—0 and 1. The numbers from 0 to 10 in binary code are:

0 = 0
1 = 1
2 = 10
3 = 11
4 = 100
5 = 101
6 = 110
7 = 111
8 = 1000
9 = 1001
10 = 10000

Binary code is used in computers to stand for figures and letters.

biogas is a *gas* that is given off when animal waste and dead plants begin to rot. Biogas contains methane gas, which can be collected and burned as a fuel.

biomass is the word we use to describe all plant and animal matter on Earth. Biomass, such as wood and dried animal dung, can be used as fuel.

bit is an electronic signal inside a *computer.* There are two sorts of bits—one (1) and zero (0). When an electric current is on, the bit is 1. When the electric current is off, the bit is 0. Groups of bits make up a *byte.*

black hole is a massive object that scientists believe may be far out in space. The black hole forms when a star collapses inward. The force of *gravity* near a black hole is so great that nothing can escape its pull. We cannot see black holes because even light rays are pulled into them.

C

camouflage is a pattern of shapes and colors that make it difficult to see a camouflaged object against its background. Some animals, such as chameleons, have camouflaged skins that help them to hide. Camouflage helps animals hide from their prey and predators.

carbohydrates are made by plants during *photosynthesis*. Starch is a carbohydrate found in foods such as corn, potatoes, yams, and rice. Table sugar and *glucose* are also carbohydrates. The carbohydrates we eat give us energy.

cartilage is a tough, flexible material found in many animal skeletons. A shark's skeleton is made up completely from cartilage.

catalyst is a *chemical* that speeds up a *chemical reaction*. We have catalysts called *enzymes* in our bodies.

cell is the smallest part of a living thing. Plants and animals are made of cells. Some simple plants and animals are made up of only one cell. Large plants and animals contain millions of cells. A cell is made up of a jellylike substance called *cytoplasm*. This surrounds a nucleus and is contained inside a membrane. There are different types of cells that do different jobs.

chemical element is any single, pure substance. The whole universe is made up of different sorts of chemicals, all mixed together in different ways. There are different families of chemicals, such as *acids* and *alkalis*.

chemical reaction changes chemicals completely to produce one or more different substances. There are three ways of making chemicals react—by mixing them together, by heating them, or by passing electricity through them.

chlorophyll is the green substance in the leaves and stems of plants. Chlorophyll is a *catalyst* that helps plants to make their own food during *photosynthesis*.

chloroplast is the working part of a plant cell that accomplishes *photosynthesis*.

class is one of the groups used by scientists to classify living things. Usually there are several classes in a *phylum*. Living things in the same class will have special similarities. Humans are in a class called *mammals*—which also contains apes, horses, whales, and mice.

climate is the usual pattern of weather for any region of the world. Climate includes the temperature and rainfall of a region.

cold blooded describes an animal that must move between warm and cold places to maintain a steady body temperature.

combustion means burning. When a substance burns, it takes in oxygen and gives out heat energy. This process is called combustion. Wood and gasoline are combustible, which means they will burn. Sand and water are noncombustible.

compound is a substance made up from atoms of different *elements*. Water is a compound made up from atoms of hydrogen and oxygen.

compression means squeezing. When a gas is squeezed, it fits into a smaller container and its pressure rises. *Liquids* are almost impossible to squeeze. Squeezing *solids* makes them bend or crack. This process is called compression.

condensation describes what happens when a *gas*, such as water vapor, turns into a *liquid* as it cools. If you breathe onto a mirror, your hot breath will condense in small water droplets on the cold mirror.

conductor is an element that carries heat, electricity, or another form of energy.

continental drift is the slow movement of land on the surface of Earth. The continents are made up from huge plates of solid rock. These float on the molten rock underneath. Over millions of years, the continents have gradually moved away from each other.

corrosion happens when solid materials are attacked by the air and other substances around them. Corrosion can eventually break solids down. Water and air corrode iron and steel, and turn them into rust. Acid rain pollution corrodes many types of building stone.

crystal is a pure, solid substance that has its own special shape. Sugar, salt, and diamonds are all crystals. Crystals of the same substance can be different sizes but they each have the same shape. Crystals grow when solutions evaporate or when molten substances freeze.

D

data means information. We collect data by measuring and observing. Data are usually written down or recorded in some other way.

decibel (dB) is a unit used to measure levels of power, usually sound. A jumbo jet is about 80 dB louder than a person speaking.

density of a substance helps to describe its heaviness. Density is measured by collecting a centimeter cube of a substance and measuring its mass in grams. Density is measured in grams per cubic centimeter (g/cm^3). The density of water is one gram per cubic centimeter ($1 g/cm^3$).

direct current (DC) is an electric current that flows steadily in one direction. Ordinary batteries supply direct current.

distillation is a way of making *liquids* more pure. Simple distillation can separate salt and water from salty water. Salty water is boiled in one container until all the water turns to steam. The steam is collected in another container where it cools to become water. The salt is left in the first container.

E

effort is the force you use to work a machine to move an object. If you use an effort to push a lever down, you can lift up a heavy load.

electrical insulator is a material that does not allow electrical energy to pass through it. Other kinds of insulators prevent the flow of either heat or sound. 1. Electric wires are covered with a plastic insulator. 2. Seals have a thick layer of fat to insulate their bodies against the cold weather.

electrode is a point in a *solution* where an electric current enters and leaves the solution.

electrolysis is a way of making chemicals change. Electricity is passed through a *solution* of a substance, called an *electrolyte*, or a solid that has been melted. The electric current starts a *chemical reaction* and new substances are made.

electromagnetic radiation is a type of energy. Radio waves, light, X rays, and gamma rays are all types of electromagnetic radiation. They all travel at the same speed—about 186,282 miles (299,792 kilometers) per second. As electromagnetic radiation travels, the energy changes back and forth from electrical energy to magnetic energy.

elements are the basic building blocks of *matter*. There are over 100 different elements. *Atoms* of these elements join together in different ways to make different sorts of matter. All elements are *chemical* elements.

endangered species are plants and animals, such as the Komodo dragon, that have almost died out. Many species are in danger because people destroy their *habitats*. *Conservation* helps many endangered species survive.

enzyme is a *catalyst* chemical found in living things. Enzymes help changes happen quickly and easily. They help us digest food, grow, move about, and think.

epiphyte is a type of plant. Epiphytes do not have roots that grow in the ground. They hang on trees and other plants for support but do not feed from them like parasites. Some mosses and ferns are epiphytes.

erosion means wearing something away. Soil is eroded when wind and water carry the soil away. Wind and water also erode rocks, but much more slowly than soil. Ice helps erosion by splitting apart cracks in rocks.

extinction means dying out. 1. Some kinds of animals, such as the dinosaur, have become extinct. 2. An extinct volcano is one that no longer spouts hot gases and molten rocks.

F

family is one of the groups used by scientists to *classify* living things. There are usually several families in an *order*. The living things in the same family have special similarities. Human beings are in the hominid family.

fertilization happens when a male sperm joins with a female egg. The fertilized egg can grow into a new living thing.

filament is a very thin thread or threadlike part or object. The wire that gives off light in a light bulb is a filament.

food chain shows how living things depend on each other for food. For example, plankton are eaten by shrimps, shrimps are eaten by fish, fish are eaten by seals, and finally, seals are eaten by killer whales.

fuse is an electrical safety device that has a piece of metal that melts when the current becomes too strong. This interrupts the circuit and turns off the flow of electricity.

G

gas is one of the three states of matter—*solid*, *liquid*, and *gas*. A gas will escape unless it is kept in a closed container. Unlike solids and liquids, gases can be compressed into a smaller space. The particles that make up a gas are much farther apart than the particles in solids and liquids.

genus is one of the groups used by scientists to sort out living things. There may be one or more genera in a family. All the living things in the same genus have special similarities. Human beings are in the genus called homo. We are the only members of this genus.

germination means sprouting. A seed sprouts and begins to grow when it has enough water, warmth, and oxygen to germinate.

glands are special parts of the bodies of living things—usually animals. Glands make substances that are used inside the body. Salivary glands make saliva that helps to keep your mouth moist. Sweat glands produce sweat to help keep your skin cool.

glucose is a type of sugar. Plants make glucose with the help of energy from the sun. Animals break down certain foods into glucose, and this is used to provide energy for their cells.

granite is a type of rock. It is formed when molten rocks deep under the ground slowly cool. Granite is hard and dense and is often made from crystals of different colors.

grasslands are large parts of Earth's surface that are covered in grass. Rain does not fall very regularly on grasslands and there are few trees.

gravitation is a force that pulls objects toward each other. If you drop something, the force of gravity makes it fall toward the ground. Earth's gravity pulls down on the mass of an object and gives it weight.

H

herbivore is an animal that eats plants. Herbivores do not eat other animals.

hertz is a unit used to measure the *frequency* of a vibrating wave. The unit is written as Hz and tells us how many times the wave vibrates each second. The frequency of sound waves that most people can hear is between 20 and 20,000 Hz. The frequency of some light waves is 750 billion hertz.

hibernation is a long, deep sleep during the cold winter. Bears, dormice, and some turtles hibernate during the cold weather when food is scarce. The hibernating animal's heart beats more slowly and the temperature of its body drops. This means the animal can live for a longer time using only energy that it has stored as body fat.

hormones are *chemicals* made by plants and animals. They act as messengers. Growth hormones tell a plant or animal to grow. Sex hormones make an animal grow into an adult male or an adult female.

humus is a part of the soil. It is made from the rotted remains of plants and animals that have been broken down by *microbes*. Plants grow well in humus because it soaks up water and allows air to pass through. It also contains *nutrients* that feed the growing plants.

hydraulic machines use a *liquid* under *pressure* to supply power to the machine. The brakes of a car are hydraulic. The brake pedal forces an oily liquid along pipes that lead to each wheel. The pressure of this liquid is the hydraulic power that works the brakes.

hydrocarbon is a substance that is made from only hydrogen and carbon. Natural gas and methane are hydrocarbons. Gasoline and diesel oil are liquid hydrocarbons. Wax is a solid hydrocarbon.

hypothalamus is a part of the brain of human beings and other *mammals*. The hypothalamus helps to control important activities in your body, such as breathing and body temperature. It also controls the pituitary gland and produces *hormones*.

I

insectivore is a living thing that eats insects. Insectivores are usually animals, such as anteaters, bats, and shrews. But some plants, such as the sundew, are also insectivores.

integrated circuits are found inside *computers* and other types of electronic equipment. They are tiny electrical circuits made on chips of a material called silicon. Electric currents follow pathways that are etched on the surface of the silicon chip.

invertebrate is an animal that does not have a backbone. Worms, mollusks, insects, and spiders are all invertebrates.

ion is an *atom* that has an electrical charge. An uncharged atom has the same number of negative *electrons* and positive *protons*. If this atom loses electrons, it becomes a positively charged ion. If it gains electrons, it becomes a negatively charged ion. Salt crystals are made from negative and positive ions, which are attracted to each other.

irrigation means watering dry soil. Irrigation pipes or channels carry water from lakes or wells to where it is needed. This helps plants and crops to grow where normal rainfall is not enough.

L

larva is one stage in the *life cycle* of some *invertebrate* animals. When an egg hatches, a larva comes out. The larva looks different from the adult. A caterpillar is the larva of a butterfly or moth. A maggot is the larva of many kinds of flies.

lattice is something that is built from parts arranged in a pattern. A lattice mast or tower is a tall structure made from long poles held together with shorter cross-pieces.

light makes it possible to see things. It is a kind of energy that travels through space. The part of that energy that we can see is called visible light. Light consists of *electromagnetic waves*. It travels through an empty space at a speed of 186,282 miles (299,792 kilometers) per second.

light-year is the distance that rays of light will travel in one year. Distances in space are measured in light-years because they are so large. A light-year is equal to 5.88 trillion miles (9.46 trillion kilometers).

lignite is a soft, brown kind of coal that was made when mud and sand were washed over layers of rotting vegetation.

M

machines help us with our work. We use them to change energy into movement to do *work*. There are six simple machines. These are *wheels* and *axles*, *levers*, *wedges*, *screws*, *pulleys*, and *inclined planes*. All these machines can make things move. Complicated machines, such as *engines*, are made from a collection of simple machines working together. Engines are used to change the energy in fuel into mechanical energy.

magma is hot, molten rock deep inside Earth. It comes to Earth's surface when a volcano erupts. When magma cools, it becomes solid and forms *igneous rocks*.

magnetic field is the force around a magnet. The field is invisible, but it can be shown in a diagram by lines drawn around the magnet. These lines show the direction of the magnetic field and where it is strongest.

magnetic pole is where a magnet's magnetic force is strongest. A magnet always has two magnetic poles—the north pole and the south pole. The same poles repel each other but opposite poles attract.

mainframe is a large, powerful computer. Unlike personal computers, mainframes are designed to be used by many people at the same time.

marsupial is a *mammal* that carries its young in a pouch on its body. When the young are born, they are very small and defenseless. They are carried in the mother's pouch until they have grown. Koala bears, opossums, and kangaroos are all marsupials.

matter is anything that has mass and takes up space. Matter can exist in three forms—*solid*, *liquid*, or *gas*.

melting is what happens when a *solid* is heated and becomes a *liquid*. It is the opposite of *freezing*.

membrane is a type of thin skin. A membrane separates two parts, such as two cells, inside the body of a living thing.

metal is an *element*. Metals conduct electricity and can be bent. Most metals are shiny and reflect light. Some have to be heated to a very high temperature to make them melt. Gold, copper, lead, and zinc are examples of metal.

metamorphosis means the complete changing of shape. Some animals change their shape when they become adults. Animals that do this are usually *invertebrates*. An example of metamorphosis is when a caterpillar changes into a *chrysalis,* which then changes into an adult butterfly.

microbe is a microscopic organism. Some *algae*, *bacteria*, *viruses*, and *yeasts* are microbes.

migration means moving from one place to another. Many animals migrate from one place to another at special times in search of food or places to breed. They may travel across land, sea, or through the air.

mineral is a solid substance that has never been alive and comes from the ground. Rocks are made from different types of minerals. Some minerals contain metals and other useful substances.

molecule is a tiny particle of matter. Molecules are made up of separate atoms joined together. They can be made of two or of thousands of atoms. A molecule of water is made up of two atoms of hydrogen joined to one atom of oxygen.

mollusk is an *invertebrate* with a soft body and no bones, which must keep its body moist. Many mollusks have hard shells, inside or outside their bodies. Mollusks form a class (group) of invertebrates.

molting is the way some animals change their skin, coat, or shell. Some vertebrate animals change their warm winter coat by losing some hair, fur, or feathers in the spring. Or they change their color by molting and then growing a new covering. Some invertebrates, such as crabs and locusts, grow larger by molting their whole outside skin and growing a new one.

N

nerve is a cell with a long fiber that carries messages around an animal's body. Messages from our eyes and ears travel through nerves to the brain.

neutron is a tiny particle found in the *nucleus* of an atom. The number of neutrons in an atom may vary.

nuclear reactor uses radioactive substances, such as *uranium*, to make heat energy. The heat energy is used to generate electricity in nuclear power stations or to drive nuclear submarines through water.

nucleus is the central part of something, around which other parts may be grouped. 1. The nucleus is the central part of all living *cells*. It contains a special chemical, called DNA, which makes each cell work properly. 2. The nucleus is also the name given to the central part of all atoms. It contains tiny particles called *protons* and *neutrons*.

O

observatory is a building that houses a telescope.

optical fiber is a long, glass tube that carries light signals. Light enters one end of the optical fiber and then travels through the core and out at the other end. Some optical fibers are only a fraction of an inch thick, but they can be several miles long.

orbit is the curved path along which one object travels around another. 1. In atoms, electrons orbit around the nucleus. 2. In the solar system, the planets orbit around the sun. The shape of Earth's orbit is an *ellipse*.

order is one of the groups used by scientists to classify living things. Usually, there are several orders in a *class*. The living things in the same order have special similarities. Human beings belong to the order of primates—which also includes chimpanzees, gorillas, and orangutans.

organs are the parts inside living things which do a special job. Inside our bodies, we have organs such as the heart, lungs, kidneys, liver, and intestines.

osmosis describes how pure *liquids* move from one side of a skin, or membrane, to the other side. The liquid always travels from a weaker solution to a stronger solution. Plants use osmosis to draw water from the ground into their roots.

ozone is a *gas* that is found in a layer of the *atmosphere*, high above the surface of Earth. It is made when strong sunlight shines on ordinary oxygen in the air. The ozone layer shields us from the harmful *ultraviolet rays* of the sun.

P

pesticide is a *chemical* used to kill harmful insects or other small pests. Pesticides usually kill only harmful animals and not harmless ones. Farmers spray pesticides on their fields to protect their crops.

phagocytes are part of the *immune system* of human beings and other mammals. They help the body guard against infection and illness. Phagocytes are single cells—sometimes called white blood *cells*—that destroy invading *bacteria* and other microbes.

photosynthesis is used by green plants to make the food they need. Energy from sunlight is trapped by a substance called *chlorophyll*. Chlorophyll helps water and carbon dioxide join together. This makes food, such as glucose and starch, for the plant.

phylum is one of the groups used by scientists to classify living things. Usually, there are several phyla in a *kingdom*. Living things in the same phylum have special similarities. Human beings are in the phylum called chordata, which includes all animals with internal skeletons.

piston is the part of a **machine** that slides back and forth inside a *cylinder*. Steam engines, bicycle pumps, and hydraulic systems use pistons and cylinders.

pixels are the spots of light on a television or computer screen that glow to make up the picture. A color picture is made up from three types of pixel—red, green, and blue. The more pixels there are on a screen, the more detail you can see in the picture.

planet is a large, natural object that travels in orbit around a *star*. Earth is one of nine planets that orbit around the sun. These are Mercury, Venus, Earth, Mars, Jupiter, Saturn, Neptune, Uranus, and Pluto. Unlike stars, planets do not give off their own light.

plankton are microscopic plants and animals. They float on the surface of the sea and lakes.

poacher is an illegal hunter of endangered animals.

pollen is the name given to the small, colored grains that you can see at the center of many flowers. Pollen grains are made in the male part of the flower. When pollen lands on the female part of a flower, it fertilizes the plant to produce seeds.

pollination is the movement of pollen from the male part of a plant to the female part of a plant. Pollen is usually carried by insects and other animals, or by the wind.

pollution is the result of harmful substances escaping into the world around us. Waste from industry, homes, and traffic can pollute the land, water, and air. Natural air pollution is caused by erupting volcanoes and forest fires.

population is the number of living things in a certain place. 1. The human population of Earth is over 6 billion. 2. The population of bees in a hive is between 50,000 and 60,000.

porous is having many small holes or pores which allow liquid to soak through.

potential energy is energy that is stored and waiting to be used.

power of a machine is the amount of work it can do. Power is measured in watts (W). One watt of power is the same as one joule of energy made or used in one second. A light bulb may use 100 watts of electrical power, and a car engine may give out 35,000 watts.

precipitation is a scientific word for rain, snow, hail, or sleet.

predator is an animal that hunts other animals for food. *Carnivores*, such as lions and spiders, are predators.

pressure is the *force* pressing on the surface of something. 1. As a diver swims deeper, there is more water above him—so the water pressure on his body is greater. 2. Atmospheric pressure is caused by the weight of air pushing down.

prey is the name given to an animal that is hunted by another animal for food. Antelopes are prey for lions, and flies are prey for spiders.

printer is a device that prints a hard copy of work done on a computer.

properties helps us to recognize similar groups of things. Simple properties are shape, color, and texture. We can discover other properties of a substance or material by testing it. For example, does it conduct electricity or bend?

protein is a special substance found in living things. Our muscles, skin, and hair are made from protein. *Enzymes* are proteins which help important chemical changes happen inside cells. We take in protein from our food.

protists are a group of simple living things. Protists are usually made up from a single cell. They include *algae* and *protozoa.*

protons are tiny particles found in the nucleus of all *atoms*. An atom usually has the same number of protons as *electrons.*

pulley is a simple *machine*. It has a wheel with a groove around its rim. A rope fits into this groove. Pulling on the rope in one direction makes a force in another direction.

pupa is a stage in the life cycle of some insects. The pupa changes into the adult. The life cycle of a moth is egg, larva (called a *caterpillar*), pupa (called a *chrysalis*), and adult.

Q

quartz is a hard mineral found in many kinds of rocks. It is often clear and colorless but can also be very colorful.

R

radiant energy is energy of light.

radiation is energy that is given out by a substance. 1. *Electromagnetic* radiation includes radio waves, light waves, ultraviolet rays, X rays, and gamma rays. 2. Radiation can also be tiny particles of matter that shoot out from radioactive atoms—alpha and beta radiation.

radioactivity is the radiation given out when parts of atoms split. Radioactive uranium atoms slowly change into atoms of lead. The radiation given off can be alpha particles, beta particles, or gamma rays.

radiocarbon dating is a method of measuring the age of rocks and fossils, bones, and even ancient cloth by measuring the amount of *radioactivity* left in the material.

rain forest is a dense forest in a wet area.

RAM (**Random Access Memory**) is computer memory that holds information for a given task.

receptors are parts of the senses of living things. Eyes and ears have receptors. There are touch receptors in your skin and taste receptors on your tongue. Receptors take in information about the outside world and send messages along nerves to the brain.

recycling means using materials again, rather than throwing them away. For example, steel from scrap cars can be recycled to make new cars. Paper, aluminum cans, and glass bottles can all be recycled. Recycling helps to conserve raw materials, such as trees and metal ores.

refraction describes how a beam of light bends as it travels from one substance into another. A magnifying glass uses refraction to bend beams of light and so make things appear larger.

reproduction is how adult living things make copies of themselves. People reproduce by giving birth to babies. Birds reproduce by laying eggs and many plants use seeds to reproduce.

resistance describes how electrical energy is changed into heat and light as it flows through a wire *conductor*. Thin wires have a higher resistance than thick wires. A thick wire might stay cool as an electric current passes through it. A thin wire made of the same material will heat up when the same electric current flows through it.

resources are materials that we take from the world around us. Coal, oil, natural gas, and metal ores are nonrenewable resources. This means that when we have used them up, they will not be replaced. Wind and wave power are renewable resources.

robot is a *machine* that follows instructions to carry out a special job. One type of robot has a *computer* that controls a tool attached to an arm. Robots are often used in factories.

ROM (**Read Only Memory**) is computer memory that holds essential information the computer needs to carry out its tasks.

root is the part of the plant that grows downward. Roots hold the plant in place and absorb water and nutrients from the soil.

S

satellite is an object that orbits around Earth or another planet. 1. The moon is a natural satellite of Earth. 2. Artificial satellites are built on Earth and put into orbit by rockets. They are used to relay radio signals or to take photographs.

screw is a simple *machine*. It is a rod with a spiral ridge, called a thread, running around its outside. Flat-head wood screws have a point at one end and a flat head at the other. They are used to hold pieces of wood together.

sedimentary rock is rock formed when layers of older rocks, plants, or animals are pressed together over long periods of time.

seeds are produced by many kinds of plants for *reproduction*. Seeds have a supply of food inside a protective shell. They can grow into new plants.

short circuit is the result when two bare wires touch each other, allowing an electric current to pass directly from one wire to the other.

solar cell can make an electric current from sunlight. A solar cell is made from a substance called *silicon* and has no moving parts. Solar cells are used to power space *satellites.*

solar energy is energy made from the sun.

solar system is made up of the sun and all the natural objects that orbit around the sun. Within our solar system, there are nine planets, the moons of the planets, asteroids, and comets.

solenoid is a coil of wire that has an *electric* current flowing through it.

solid is a body of *matter* that does not change shape. The molecules in a solid are held together by an electrical force.

solute is a substance that dissolves in a *liquid.* Salt is a solute when it dissolves in water. Solutes can be *solids, liquids,* or *gases.*

solution is the result of dissolving a substance, called a *solute,* in a *liquid.* Salt dissolves in water to make salt solution.

sound is produced by vibrations from an object. Sound travels faster through liquids and solids than it travels through air. Most of the sounds you hear have traveled through the air. Sound travels 1,116 feet (340 meters) per second through air at sea level at a temperature of 59 °F (15 °C). The speed of sound is much slower than the speed of light.

species is one of the groups used by scientists to classify living things. Living things in the same species are able to breed with each other, and their young grow up to look like the parents. Human beings are a species, giant pandas are another species, and tigers are yet another species.

spectrum is a range of similar things. 1. The band of colors that you see when a ray of white light is split up as it shines through a prism is a spectrum. The colors of the rainbow make up a spectrum of colors. 2. The electromagnetic spectrum includes different types of waves—from radio waves to gamma rays. The frequency of the waves increases from one end of the spectrum to the other.

sphere is any object, such as a globe or an orange, that is round like a ball.

spinal cord is a thick bundle of nerves that run down the back inside the backbone and carries messages from the brain to the rest of the body.

spore is a tiny *cell,* or group of cells, used for *reproduction.* Fungi, some *bacteria,* and protists and certain plants, such as ferns and mosses, produce spores. Plant spores are often scattered by the wind. Each spore can grow into a new plant. Unlike *seeds,* spores do not contain a store of food.

star is a large ball of glowing gases in the sky. Stars release huge amounts of energy in the form of both light and heat. The sun is a star. It is the center of our *solar system.*

stomata are tiny holes in the bottom surface of leaves, Gases and water vapor enter and leave the plant through the stomata.

T

temperature describes how hot or cold a substance is. Hot substances have higher temperatures than cold substances. Temperature is measured in degrees Fahrenheit (°F) or degrees Celsius (°C). Ice melts to a liquid at 32 °F, which is the same as 0 °C. Water boils to steam at 212 °F, or 100 °C.

tension is a *force* that is caused by an object being stretched.

terminal means "end." A battery terminal is the end of a battery where a wire is joined to make a connection.

thermometer is used to measure *temperature*. One type of thermometer is a thin, glass tube containing a liquid, which is usually mercury. As the temperature rises, the liquid expands up the tube. The temperature is measured by reading a scale marked along the side of the thermometer tube

tissue is the material that makes up the different parts of living things. Tissue is a collection of similar *cells* that behave in similar ways. Skin, muscle, and bark are different types of tissue.

transmitter sends something from one place to another. 1. A radio transmitter can send signals—*electromagnetic waves*—to radio receivers in another town or country. 2. A loudspeaker transmits sounds. 3. Some mosquitoes transmit diseases by carrying *microbes* from one person to another.

transpiration is the name given to the way that plants lose water. The water is usually lost as vapor that passes out through tiny holes, or *stomata*, in the leaves. Transpiration helps plants move *nutrients* up from the roots and through the stems to the leaves.

tropical rain forests grow in the tropics where the climate is hot and wet. This type of forest is very dense, with more *species* of trees than any other forest. About half the world's species of plants and animals live here. The tallest trees may grow to be as tall as 200 feet (60 meters).

troposphere is the layer of the *atmosphere* where all the gases needed by living things on Earth are.

tundra is a type of *habitat* that is found in the northern parts of Earth. No trees grow there, and plants grow for only a short period during the year. The soil is frozen for the rest of the time.

tungsten is a thin coil of metal that gives off light and gets very hot when an *electric current* passes through it.

turbine is a *machine* that turns to make mechanical energy. A *liquid* or a *gas* flows through the turbine and spins a shaft fitted with curved blades. Turbines are used in jet engines and power stations.

U

ultraviolet ray is an invisible form of light. The sun is the major source of ultraviolet rays. They can make pale human skin become darker in sunlight.

uranium is a silver-white, radioactive metal that is used as a source of nuclear energy. It is a chemical element.

V

vaccination is the giving of vaccine medicine to protect against disease.

valve is a door that controls the flow of a *liquid* or a *gas* along a pipe. 1. An animal's heart contains valves to make the blood flow the right way. 2. Oil and gas pipe lines are fitted with valves. Boilers are fitted with safety valves that open automatically if the steam *pressure* becomes dangerously high.

vapor is water boiled away as a gas.

vegetarian is a person who does not eat meat, fish, or some other animal foods.

vein is a tube known as a blood vessel, that carries blood to the heart from other parts of the body. Arteries, another kind of blood vessel, carry blood from the heart throughout the body. Microscopic capillaries, the third form of blood vessels, connect arteries and veins.

ventilation describes how air moves into and through a space. 1. We can ventilate a room by opening a window. 2. We ventilate our lungs by breathing in and out.

vertebrates are the group of animals that have backbones. They include human beings, mice, snakes, and most fish.

vibration is a rapid or continuous movement to and fro or up and down. The strings in a piano or guitar vibrate. Sound waves spread out from the vibrating strings.

virus is the smallest type of *microbe*. There are many different types of viruses. They cause diseases by reproducing inside healthy *cells* and destroying them. Many scientists say that viruses are not actually alive.

vitamin is a chemical substance that living things need to stay healthy. Animals, such as human beings, must regularly take in small amounts of different vitamins in their food. Fresh fruit and vegetables contain many important vitamins.

volt is a unit of measurement used in *electrical circuits*. It describes the strength of the push that moves an electric current around a circuit. The kind of single-cell battery used in a flashlight has a voltage of 1.5 volts. Doubling the voltage will double the current in a simple circuit.

volume describes how much room or space is taken up by something. Volume also describes how loud a sound is. A large volume of sound means a loud sound.

W

warbler is any of several small songbirds. Most warblers have brightly colored feathers.

wavelength is the distance between the top of one wave of light and the top of the next wave.

weight is the force of *gravity* pulling down on an object. The weight of an object becomes smaller as it moves away from a planet. The gravity on Earth is six times greater than the gravity on the moon. An object, or *mass*, that weighs 60 pounds (27 kilograms) on Earth weighs only 10 pounds (4.5 kilograms) on the moon. In space, where gravitational force is too weak, objects have no weight.

woodland is a type of *habitat*. Woodland is made up from deciduous trees, which lose their leaves in winter. The trees in woodlands grow farther apart than the trees in forests. Sunlight can reach the ground where grasses and other plants can grow.

work is done when a *force* moves an object. If you pull on a rope and pulley, you can lift a heavy load.

X

X ray is a type of light that we cannot see. It is part of the electromagnetic *spectrum.* X rays are used to make photographs of the insides of things, such as the skeleton of a person.

Y

yeast is a single-celled fungus. It reproduces by splitting in two or by forming a bud which breaks away to become a new cell. Yeasts make useful enzymes that break down sugar and starch.

Answers

Here are the answers to some of the questions you have been asked in your *Young Scientist* set.

1 Living world/Plants, page 14

Your chart of the five major kingdoms should look like this:

Animals	Plants	Fungi	Protists	Monera
tiger	pine tree	oyster mushroom	amoeba	cocci
owl	convolvulus			
snake				
spider				
sea anemone				

7 Space technology/Computers, page 69

In the binary system, the next column after eights is sixteens (2×8).

7 Space technology/Computers, page 70

If 3 transporters each carry 8 cars, there will be **24** cars altogether.

7 Space technology/Computers, page 71

If a jug holds enough lemonade for 6 drinks, you will need **6** full jugs to serve 36 children.

7 Space technology/Computers, page 71

If a bus can carry 40 people, **6** buses will be needed to carry 240 people to a football match.

7 Space technology/Computers, page 77

If you choose the right answers in the maze, you will arrive at the **Cannotbe** animal.

7 Space technology/Computers, page 81

If you work out 5 × 9 by putting down your fifth finger, you can count 4 fingers on your left hand and 5 fingers on your right hand. So the answer is **45**.

7 Space technology/Computers, page 82

Your number puzzle should look like this:

7	2		1	5	4
9	0	3		5	0
5	0	8	2		
	1	8	0	0	
1					8
6	9		3	2	6

7 Space technology/Computers, page 100

If you follow the flow chart, the answer will be **45**.

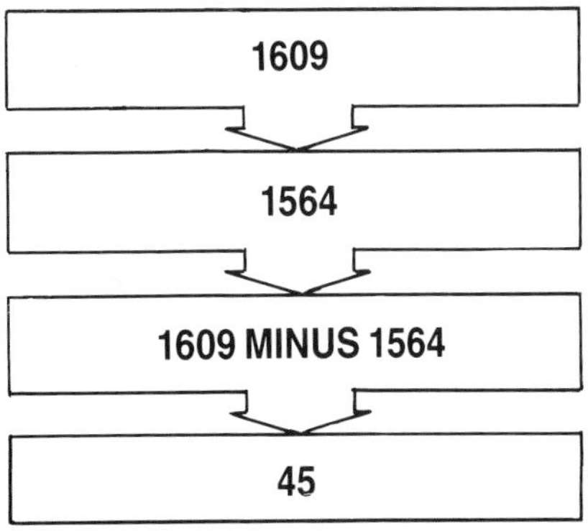

Topic webs

Have you ever been asked to carry out a project on a special topic? On the next 10 pages there are five topic webs. In a topic "web" you can follow a series of linked boxes laid out like a web. Each box contains information to help you discover more about a particular theme, or topic. Topic webs show how you can explore lots of different ideas around a main theme. The five topics you will find here are Color, Growth, Weather, Technology, and Movement. Next to each topic web is a list of questions. You can use the topic web to help you answer all of the questions.

Choosing a topic

Think carefully about what you have read in your *Young Scientist* set. Can you remember which topics interested you most? Now look at each of the five topic webs and decide which of the topics you would most like to explore.

Where do you begin?

Before you begin to look at your topic web, make sure you have paper and a pen or pencil. You will need these to write down all the interesting facts that you will discover. Now turn to the topic web that you have chosen. You will find the name of the topic in a yellow oval, in the center of the web. This box is your starting point. To find out about your chosen topic, follow one of the lines leading away from the yellow oval. You will soon reach a blue oval. Inside this blue oval is the name of one of your *Young Scientist* books. Make sure you have this book in front of you before you begin.

Using a topic web

Follow one of the lines leading away from the blue oval, until you reach an orange box. Take your *Young Scientist* book and look up the page numbers shown in the orange box. Can you find any information on the topic you have chosen? Remember to look at the list of questions next to the topic web. Can this page help you to answer one of those questions? Always remember to make a note of what you find out. You can keep all these notes neatly in your notebook.

Now go back to the blue oval and check to see if there are any more orange boxes connected to it. If there are, look up the page numbers in those boxes, too.

When you have finished, go back to the yellow oval and start again by looking for a new blue oval. Continue until you have looked up all the information in all the orange boxes.

Displaying your topic

When you have finished using the topic web, you may like to turn your notes into something that you can display. Read through the notes in your notebook and think of the best way to present your information. Perhaps you can make a wall chart or a mini-book. Perhaps you would like to paint a picture.

Can you make your own topic web?

When you have finished your topic, you may like to make your own topic web. Think of a new topic that interests you and then use the index in this volume to write out your own topic web. You may like to show a friend how your topic web works.

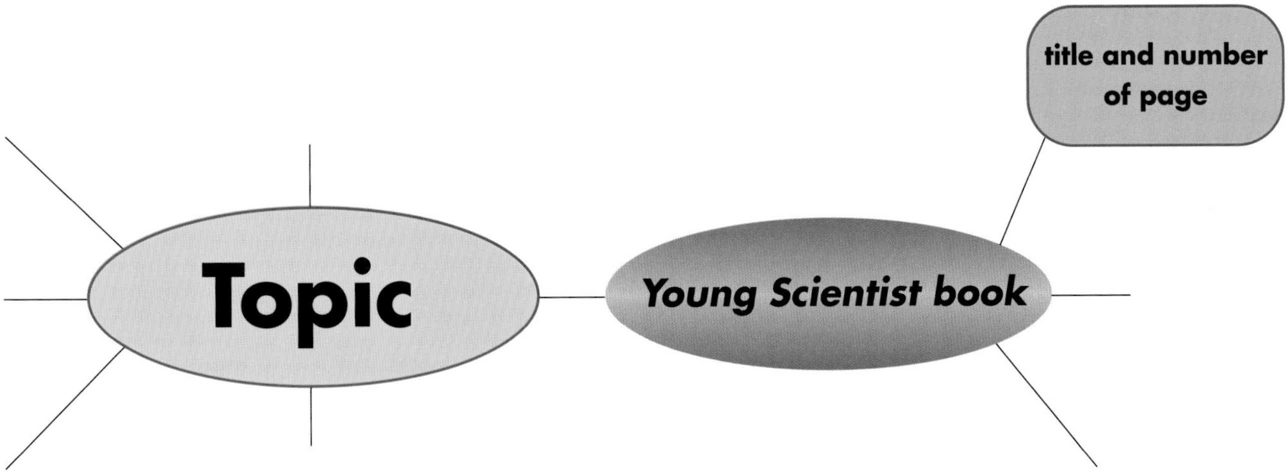

Finding out about growth

1. How long can some seeds lie dormant before they grow?

2. What do animals need to grow?

3. What do plants need to grow?

4. How many stages are there in the life cycle of a butterfly?

5. How long does it take for tadpoles to grow legs?

6. Do all your cells grow at the same time?

7. How fast is the world's population growing?

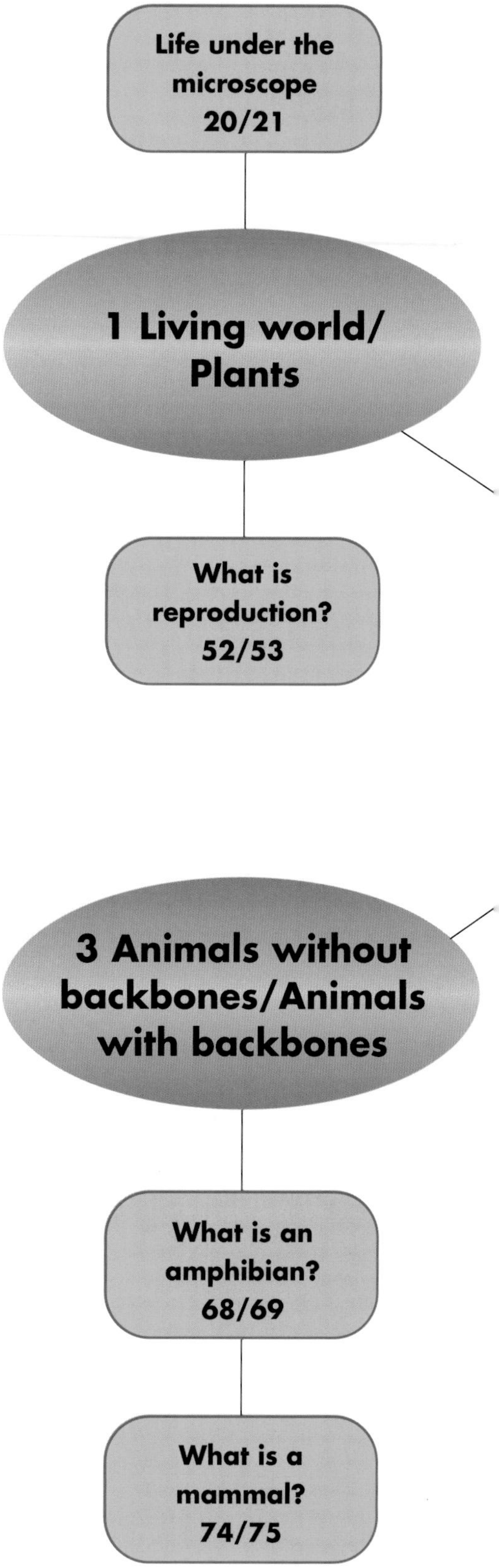

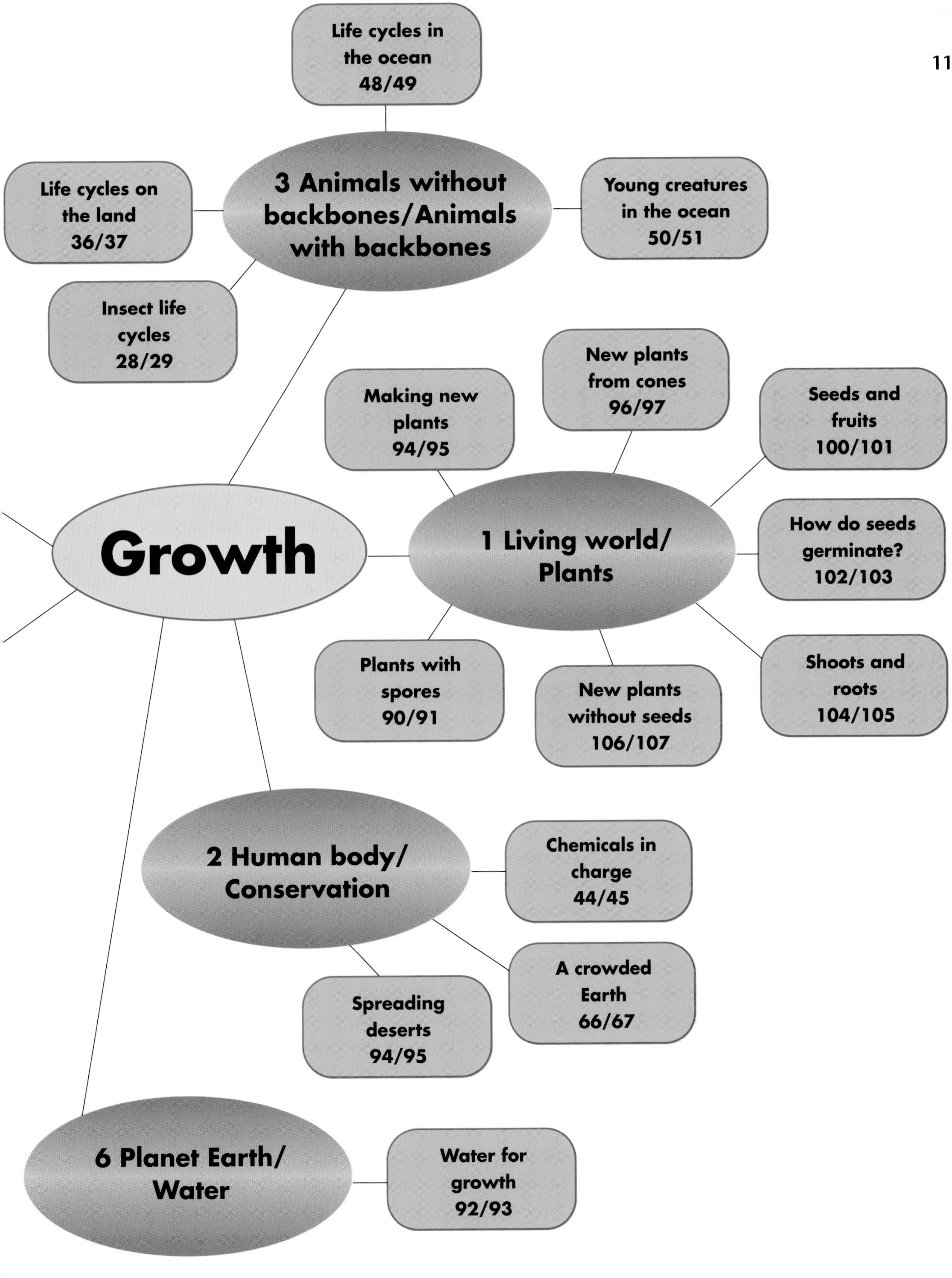
Growth
3 Animals without backbones/Animals with backbones
Life cycles in the ocean 48/49
Life cycles on the land 36/37
Young creatures in the ocean 50/51
Insect life cycles 28/29
1 Living world/ Plants
Making new plants 94/95
New plants from cones 96/97
Seeds and fruits 100/101
How do seeds germinate? 102/103
Shoots and roots 104/105
New plants without seeds 106/107
Plants with spores 90/91
2 Human body/ Conservation
Chemicals in charge 44/45
A crowded Earth 66/67
Spreading deserts 94/95
6 Planet Earth/ Water
Water for growth 92/93

Finding out about color

1. Why are animals different colors?
2. Which colors mean “stay away” to other animals?
3. Why is a sunflower yellow?
4. Why do things look colorless in the moonlight?
5. What colors are the dots on a television screen?
6. When do we use color in a chemistry laboratory?

Defenses
56/57

1 Living world/ Plants

The television camera
46/47

8 Communication/ Energy

Receiving television
48/49

2 Human body/ Conservation

The amazing eye
34/35

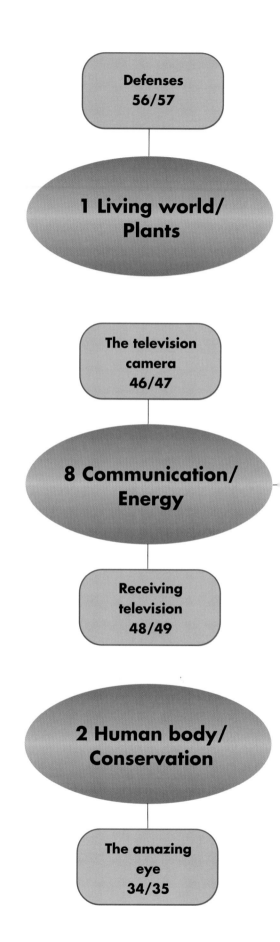

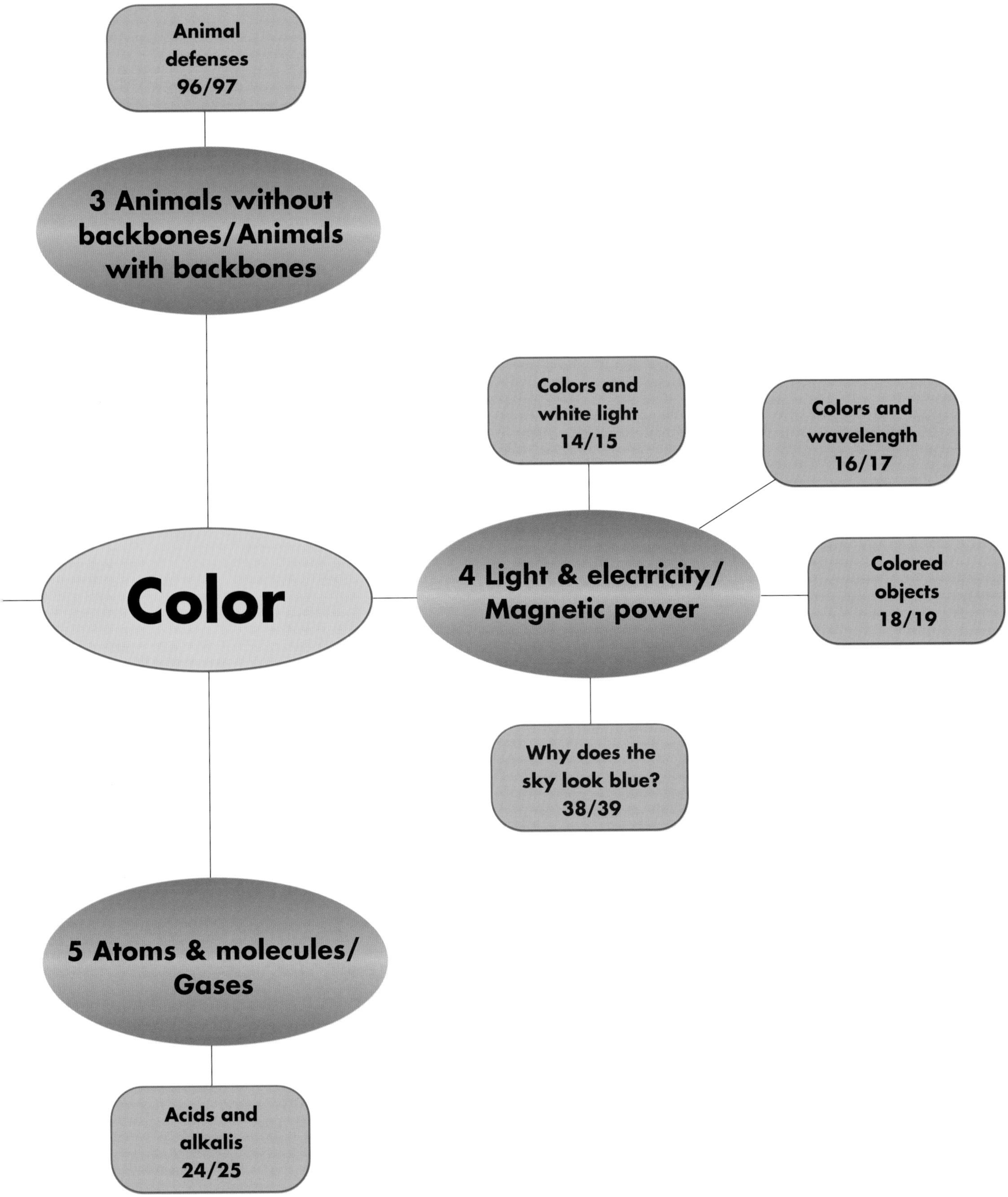
Animal defenses 96/97
3 Animals without backbones/Animals with backbones
Colors and white light 14/15
Colors and wavelength 16/17
Color
4 Light & electricity/ Magnetic power
Colored objects 18/19
Why does the sky look blue? 38/39
5 Atoms & molecules/ Gases
Acids and alkalis 24/25

Finding out about technology

1. How can lasers be used in hospitals?
2. What is the usual name for an integrated circuit?
3. What are the main uses of satellites?
4. When did scientists first split the nucleus of an atom?
5. Could you live without electricity?
6. Name two modern materials that help us to build tall buildings.
7. What is a bar code?
8. How can magnets help us to recycle metals?
9. What new substances are made when an electric current is passed through a salt solution?
10. How are robots used in industry?

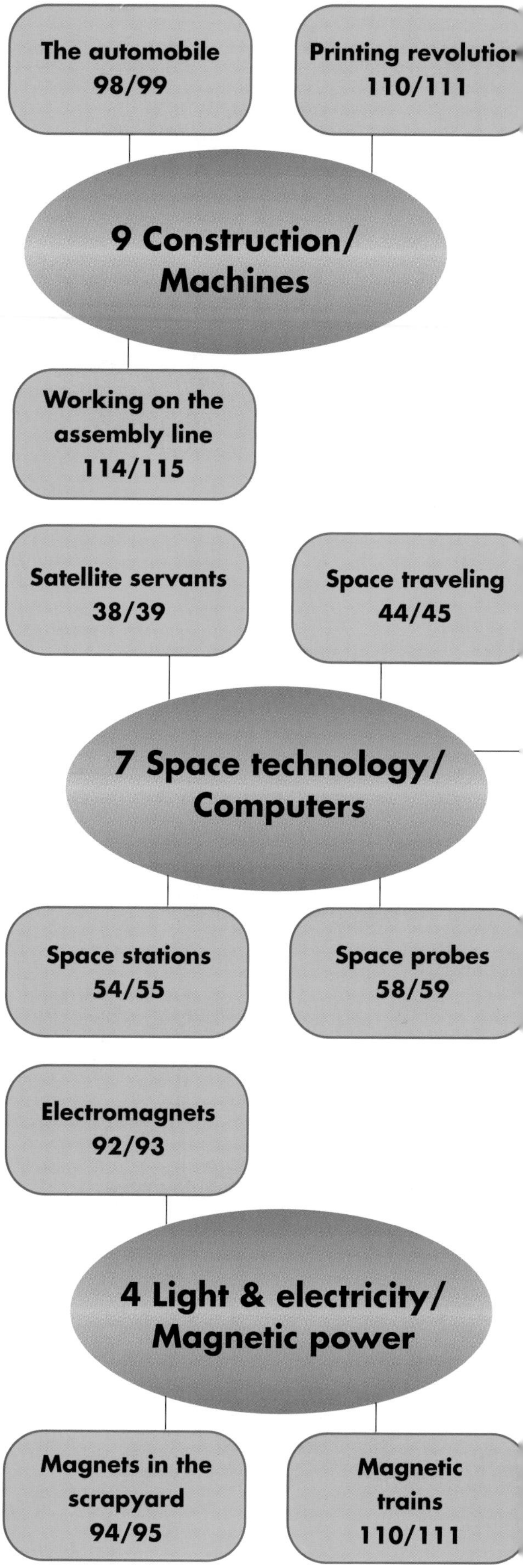

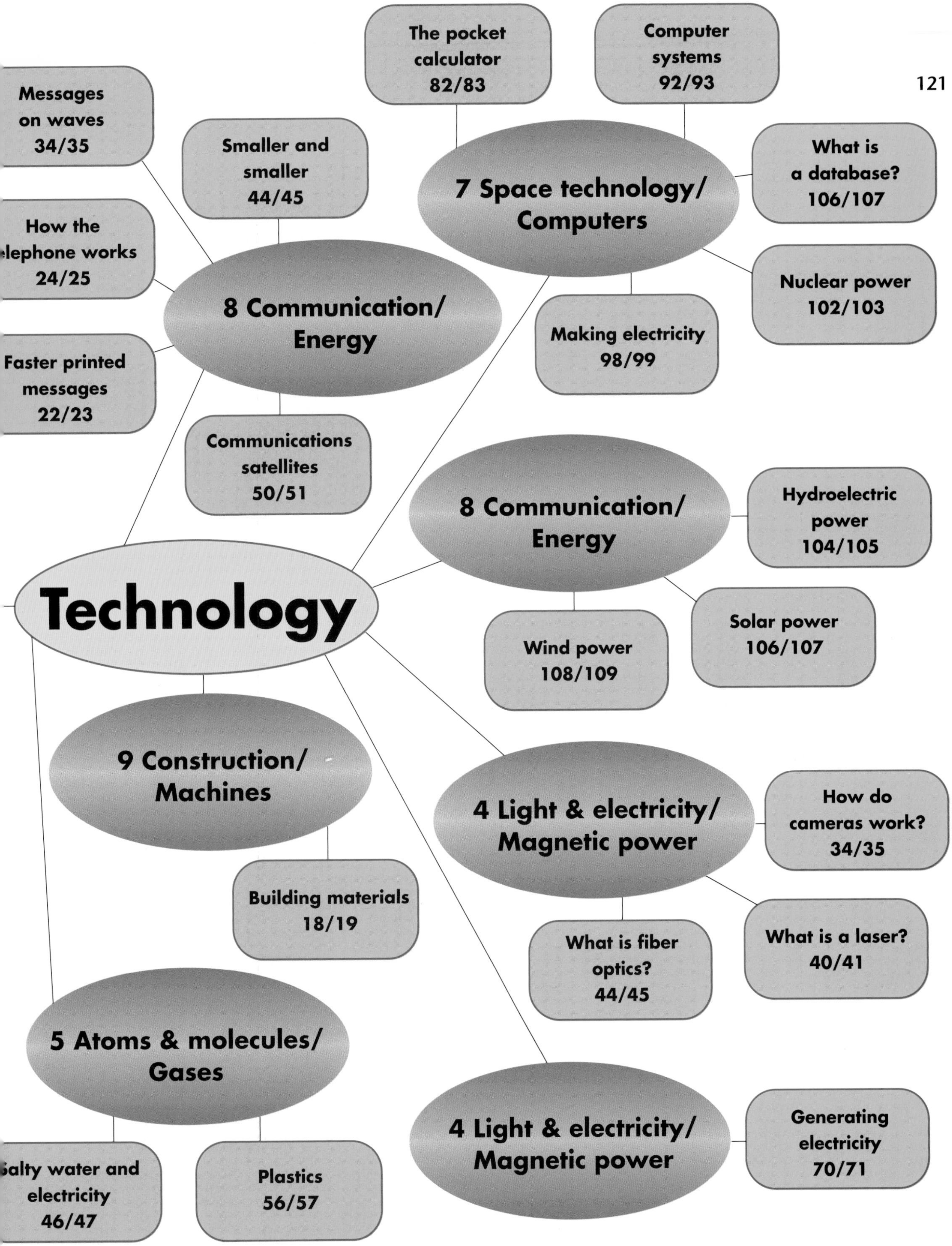
Technology
8 Communication/ Energy
Messages on waves 34/35
Smaller and smaller 44/45
How the lephone works 24/25
Faster printed messages 22/23
Communications satellites 50/51
7 Space technology/ Computers
The pocket calculator 82/83
Computer systems 92/93
What is a database? 106/107
Nuclear power 102/103
Making electricity 98/99
8 Communication/ Energy
Hydroelectric power 104/105
Solar power 106/107
Wind power 108/109
9 Construction/ Machines
Building materials 18/19
4 Light & electricity/ Magnetic power
How do cameras work? 34/35
What is a laser? 40/41
What is fiber optics? 44/45
5 Atoms & molecules/ Gases
alty water and electricity 46/47
Plastics 56/57
4 Light & electricity/ Magnetic power
Generating electricity 70/71

Finding out about movement

1. Can water move uphill?

2. Do beetles have muscles like us?

3. Do you have to think before you move?

4. Which fish moves like a snake?

5. How could you lift a car?

6. Which machines use wheels?

7. How long does it take for Earth to move around the sun?

8. In which parts of the world do earthquakes occur?

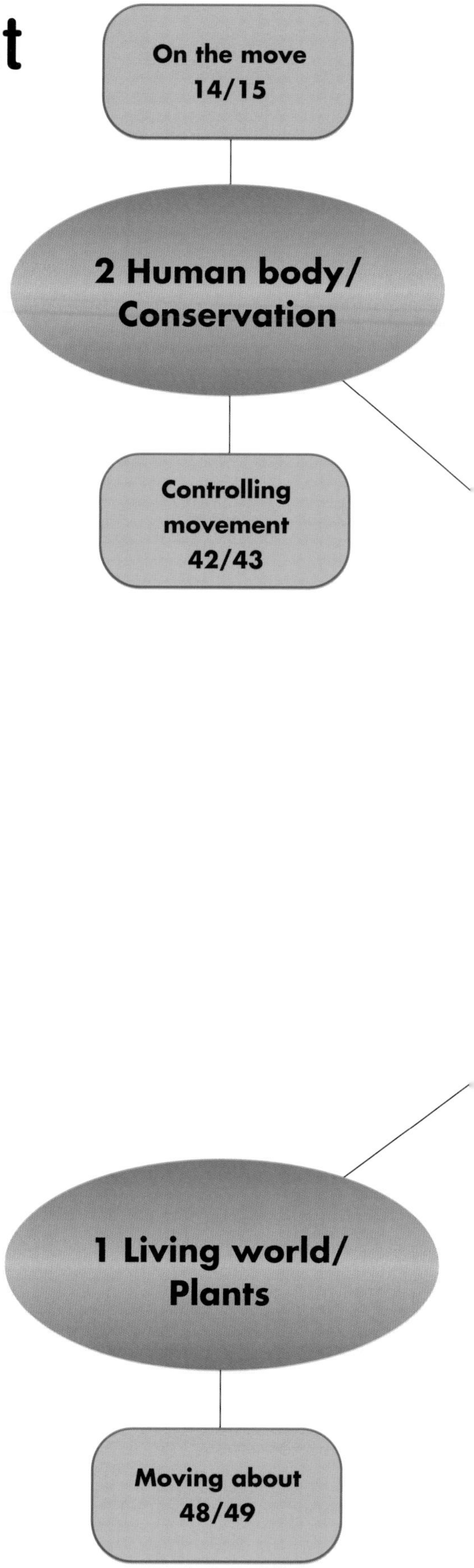

Movement

3 Animals without backbones/Animals with backbones

- How do birds fly? 82/83
- How do fish swim? 84/85
- nimal travelers 94/95

6 Planet Earth/ Water

- Land on the move 16/17
- Making mountains 18/19
- When Earth shakes 20/21
- Why does the ocean move? 28/29
- The water merry-go-round 66/67
- Pushing through water 100/101

9 Construction/ Machines

- Friction 70/71
- Screws are machines 80/81
- Pulleys—simple and complex 88/89
- Wheels and axles 82/83

7 Space technology/ Computers

- The solar system 20/21
- The planets 22/23
- Space traveling 44/45

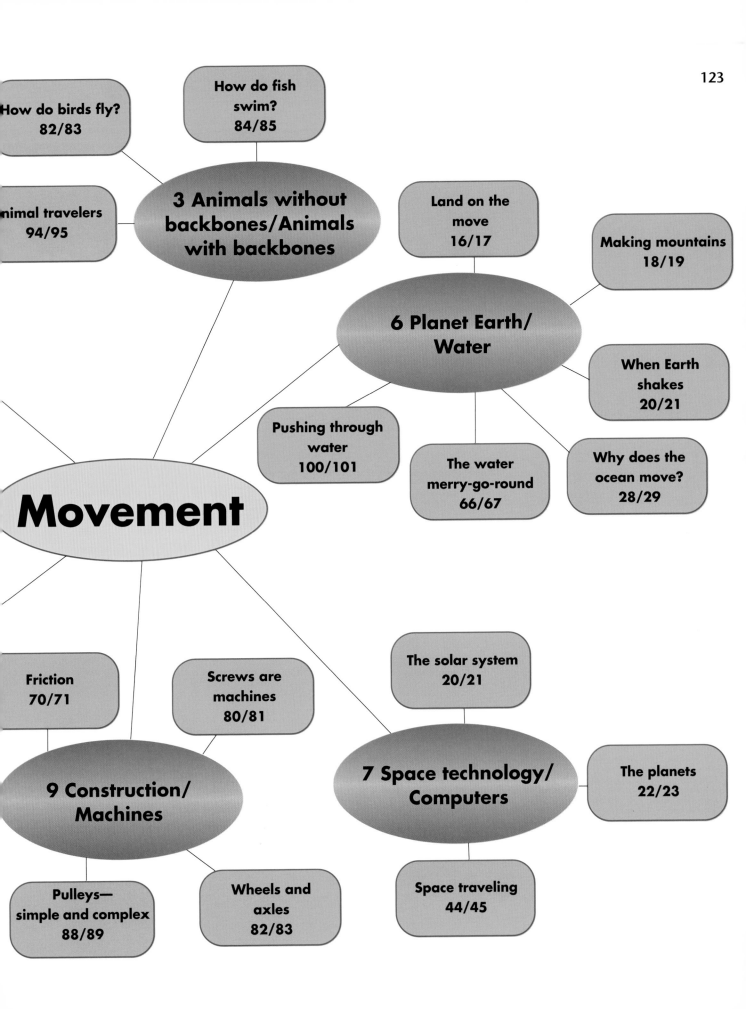

Finding out about weather

1. How hot is lightning?

2. Where do clouds come from?

3. When could the wind blow your house down?

4. How do birds stay cool?

5. Is there weather on the moon?

6. Why might the seas rise?

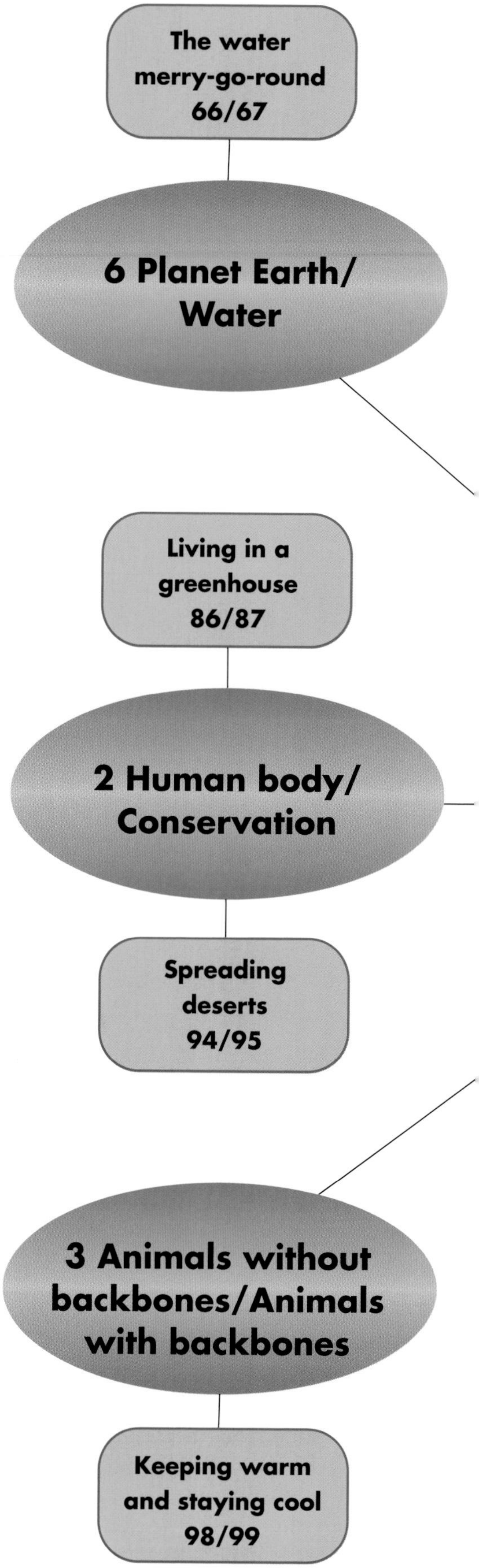
The water merry-go-round 66/67
6 Planet Earth/ Water
Living in a greenhouse 86/87
2 Human body/ Conservation
Spreading deserts 94/95
3 Animals without backbones/Animals with backbones
Keeping warm and staying cool 98/99

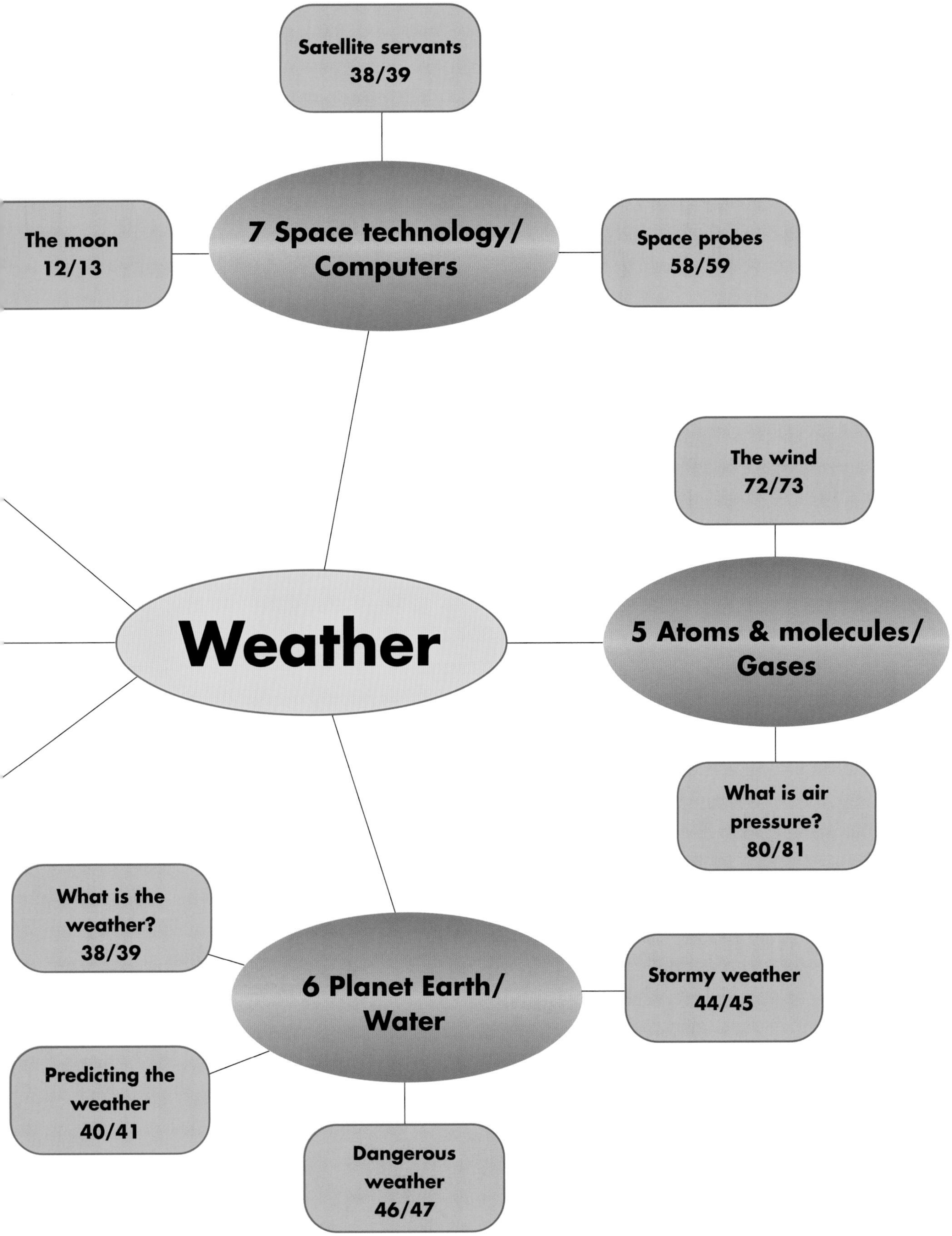
Satellite servants
38/39
The moon
12/13
7 Space technology/
Computers
Space probes
58/59
The wind
72/73
Weather
5 Atoms & molecules/
Gases
What is air
pressure?
80/81
What is the
weather?
38/39
6 Planet Earth/
Water
Stormy weather
44/45
Predicting the
weather
40/41
Dangerous
weather
46/47

Acknowledgements

The publishers of **World Book's** *Young Scientist* acknowledge the following photographers, publishers, agencies, and corporations for photographs used in this volume.

Cover	© PhotoDisc, Inc.; WORLD BOOK photo
2/3	© PhotoDisc, Inc.
6/7	WORLD BOOK photo
8/9	ZEFA Picture Library
14/15	NASA/JPL
16/17	© Schimmelpfennig, ZEFA Picture Library; © Ed Bock, The Stock Market
18/19	© Lawrence Migdale, Photo Researchers; © ZEFA Picture Library
22/23	© Peter Woloszynski

Illustrated by

Martin Aitchinson
Nigel Alexander
Hemesh Alles
Martyn Andrews
Sue Barclay
Richard Berridge
John Booth
Lou Bory
Maggie Brand
Stephen Brayfield
Bristol Illustrators
Colin Brown
Estelle Carol
David Cook
Marie DeJohn
Richard Deverell
Farley, White and Veal
Sheila Galbraith
Peter Geissler
Jeremy Gower
Kathie Kelleher
Stuart Lafford
John Lobban
Louise Martin
Annabel Milne
Yoshi Miyake
Donald Moss
Eileen Mueller Neill
Teresa O'Brien
Paul Perreault
Roberta Polfus
Jeremy Pyke
Trevor Ridley
Barry Rowe
Don Simpson
Gary Slater
Lawrie Taylor
Gwen Tourret
Pat Tourret
Peter Visscher
David Webb
Gerald Whitcomb
Matthew White
Lynne Willey